Creative Singlehood and Pastoral Care

Creative Pastoral Care and Counseling Series
 Editor: Howard J. Clinebell
 Associate Editor: Howard W. Stone

Creative Singlehood
and
Pastoral Care

John R. Landgraf

Fortress Press Philadelphia

Library of Congress Cataloging in Publication Data

Landgraf, John R.
    Creative singlehood and pastoral care.

    (Creative pastoral care and counseling series)
    Bibliography: p.
    1. Single people.   2. Church work with single people.
I. Title. II. Series.
HQ800.L33   305'.90652   82-7439
ISBN 0-8006-0569-1   AACR2

9593C82   Printed in the United States of America   1–569

To Anne
whose mastery of singlehood paved the way
for this happily single man to become even happier unsingle
and to J. P.
whose loving goads helped me keep writing

Contents

Series Foreword

Let me share with you some of the hopes that are in the minds of those of us who helped to develop this series—hopes that relate directly to you as the reader. It is our desire and expectation that these books will be of help to you in developing better working tools as a minister-counselor. We hope that they will do this by encouraging your own creativity in developing more effective methods and programs for helping people live life more fully. It is our intention in this series to affirm the many things you have going for you as a minister in helping troubled persons—the many assets and resources from your religious heritage, your role as the leader of a congregation, and your unique relationship to individuals and families throughout the life cycle. We hope to help you reaffirm the power of the pastoral by the use of fresh models and methods in your ministry.

The aim of the series is not to be comprehensive with respect to topics but rather to bring innovative approaches to some major types of counseling. Although the books are practice-oriented, they also provide a solid foundation of theological and psychological insights. They are written primarily for ministers (and those preparing for the ministry) but we hope that they will also prove useful to other counselors who are interested in the crucial role of spiritual and value issues in all helping relationships. In addition we hope that the series will be useful in seminary courses, clergy support groups, continuing education workshops, and lay befriender training.

This is a period of rich new developments in counseling and psychotherapy. The time is ripe for a flowering of creative methods and insights in pastoral care and counseling. Our expectation is that this series will stimulate grass-roots creativity as innovative methods and programs come alive for you. Some of the major thrusts discussed in this series include a new awareness of the unique contributions of the theologically trained counselor, the liberating power of the human potentials orientation, an appreciation of the pastoral-care function of the ministering congregation, the importance of humanizing systems and institutions as well as close relationships, the importance of pastoral *care* (not just counseling), the many opportunities for caring ministries throughout the life cycle, the deep changes in male-female relationships, and the new psychotherapies such as Gestalt therapy, Transactional Analysis, educative counseling, and crisis methods. Our hope is that this series will enhance your resources for your ministry to persons by opening doorways to understanding of these creative thrusts in pastoral care and counseling.

In this volume John Landgraf explores *singlehood*—an area of pastoral care and counseling which will become increasingly crucial in the years ahead. In the past, an appropriate emphasis on creative marriage has been accompanied by an unfortunate underemphasis on creative singlehood. As the number of single adults continues to increase in our society, it is imperative that pastoral counselors and other growth-enabling professionals develop the understanding and skills required to respond to their needs.

John Landgraf brings some rich resources to the task of exploring singlehood. Since 1975 he has been Director of Career Counseling at The Center for the Ministry in Oakland, California, an agency for personal growth and career development of church professional leaders. Prior to his present job, John was for four years a pastoral counselor on the staff of the Interfaith Counseling Service of Scottsdale, Arizona. These positions have given him wide experience in counseling with single persons, both ordained and nonordained. In this book John blends insights gained from his personal experiences of marriage, divorce, singlehood, and remarriage with his professional expertise in counseling with single persons.

A central motif of this book is the view that increasing one's effectiveness in ministry with singles depends on deepening one's understanding of singlehood. This understanding must recognize both the commonalities and the differences of the four types of singleness—single by death, divorce, default, choice. In the pages that follow, each of these types is explored and illuminated by case examples.

Singlehood is seen by the author as involving both difficult problems (exacerbated by our marriage-oriented society which makes "being married" the norm) *and* significant potentialities for creative living. There is a down-to-earth realism about John Landgraf's discussion of the stresses and problems singles face—e.g. lonesomeness and sex. Throughout the book there is an awareness of the impact of the larger society on singles, including the dual standard of female/male singleness which puts special pressures on single women.

The potential value of this book is enhanced by the fact that it is written so as to be useful for two groups of readers—single persons themselves and those doing caring and counseling with singles. This is a book that a pastor can loan to newly single persons to help them understand their crises and learn to handle constructively the many complex issues such crises bring. The book can be used productively as a study-discussion guide in a creative singlehood group or in a grief growth group for those who have lost spouses by death or divorce. The book is a valuable resource for pastors and other counselors who wish to increase their effectiveness as nurturers of healing and growth in the lives of single persons. The chapter on "Launching a Singles Ministry" offers a variety of practical suggestions for developing church programs designed to help meet the special needs of singles.

As one who has been unsingle for over half my life, I found that reading the manuscript of this book was a particularly learningful experience! If you are married or in some other ongoing committed relationship, I suspect that encountering this book will enhance dramatically your empathy for single persons in our contemporary society. The author encourages unsingle persons to read the book *as if* they were single, so that the single experience may come alive for them. I found this very difficult, to say the least. But the struggle of trying to do so made me more aware of the chasm between the single and unsingle experience, a chasm which must be bridged if an unsingle person is to work growthfully with singles.

I particularly appreciated (because of my own biases, I suspect) John Landgraf's robust emphasis on the growth possibilities of singlehood. He describes one growth task—becoming "well-married to oneself"—as the key to being either creatively single or creatively unsingle. I find his discussion of this principle useful personally as I struggle with one of my current growth issues—learning to be more centered, at home, and joyful with myself, a task which involves defining my own identity more clearly and in ways not fused with my spouse's identity.

I hope that you will use this book to encounter and enrich your own sense of "singleness," whether you are single or married. As the author makes clear, this process enables one to develop more creative closeness with others. Most important, I trust that the book will help you, as it did this reader, "celebrate our child-of-Godness" more fully.

HOWARD CLINEBELL

Preface

I was married for fourteen years. The first seven years were good. The next seven were not so good, although I learned much more about myself during the not-so-good years than I did in the previous seven. Then, following a divorce that simply had to happen in order for each of us to mature, I was single for six years. The first three were not so good, the next three very good. This time I learned more from the good years. Maybe that's progress. Anyway, I came to like being single. I came to believe in singlehood, even in the necessity of singlehood along the path to maturity. I also came to believe, in a new way, in marriage, so much so that two years ago I married again, this time with eyes wide open. But I still believe in singlehood—and in divorce. Yes, there is a time and place for divorce, a time when nothing else will do. I am glad I became divorced. I am glad I had six years as a single. I am glad for my new marriage.

While all this was happening I continued to work at my profession, that of a pastoral counselor specializing of all things in marriage counseling, family therapy, and career guidance! That is still my profession, only now I am more skilled and at ease in it, with fewer hidden agendas to pursue along the way. I mention this because in my practice nowadays I am seeing many Protestant ministers who are single, most often by divorce, and I am concerned about their apparent eagerness to remarry as soon as possible. Male clergy seem particularly uncomfortable with being single.

That's a bit about me and my life.

What about you? You may be single by divorce, as I was, or

single by choice, or by your spouse's death, or by some kind of default, perhaps having simply never met an appropriate person to court as a potential mate. Actually most singles choose their singlehood, whether consciously or unconsciously. It is also possible to relinquish singlehood, if that is one's goal, although in our inequitable society heterosexual women from midlife on are faced with decreasing options. Many of you, single or not, may be seriously interested in counseling and caring for single adults from a pastoral perspective. In either case, whether you are single or want to minister to singles—or both—this book is for you. Its purpose is twofold.

The book is intended primarily for people called to minister to the singles who populate our world in increasing numbers. It can help pastors counsel and care more effectively, with greater understanding of what singlehood is and can be. It offers specific suggestions on how ministers can be useful to singles in ways that make theological sense and speak to their developmental needs.

A friend of mine who pastors a local congregation recently engaged in a demographic survey of his constituency in connection with a stewardship campaign. One of his discoveries, to his surprise and chagrin, was that nearly two-thirds of that church's membership was nonmarried. The minister was surprised because he had wrongfully assumed marrieds to be the "staple" in the congregation's corporate life style. His chagrin was due to the sudden awareness that during his years there, nothing had been planned with singles in mind—no sermon, church school elective, social event, conference, or retreat. This book speaks to such a vacuum in the life of many churches.

A secondary purpose of the book has to do with my concern for single adults. If you are single, I'd like to help you be more comfortable and at home with single living, whatever its cause or origin. Maybe you've been married but your marriage has now been ravaged as if by fire. You have been subjected to an unwanted divorce; your marital house has burned down. That's sad; but what is, *is*. The question is, how now do you rise from the ashes? I know from personal experience how hard it is to attend to a head cold while your house is burning down; one does not coddle a minor ache while being devastated by an overwhelming pain. But once your house lies in smoldering ashes, you'd better pay attention to that minor cold or it may turn into pneumonia. For surviving singles now eager to address their sniffles, sneezes, and coughs, and learn how to build themselves a new "house" to live in, this book contains some ideas that may be of interest. For singles who already feel healthy and at home in their singlehood, I congratulate you and hope that reading what I have to say here will not only help you sustain your sense of wholeness but also furnish you with tools you can use in helping others.

Finally, I encourage the unsingle reader to read as if single. Approached from that perspective, this book can help the single experience come alive for you in a way that an ordinary onlooker might miss.

1. The Dynamics of Singlehood

Certain kinds of people are neither single nor married, in the sense in which these terms are ordinarily used. The most obvious example is the little child who is appropriately a part of some form of small community without which it would die. Normally this community includes at least the twosome of mother and child, whose relationship involves deep mutual attachment and life under one roof. A second example is the person who chooses a special form of religious life, as in the case of Roman Catholic orders. Such persons are single in the technical sense, yet they usually have a family-like relationship with their particular community, often for life. Third, our present society includes many people who have life styles that resist labeling: the live-in lovers who are committed to one another, coown property, and bear children but do not formally marry; the elderly couple who share a home and take vacations together but avoid the economic penalties associated with legalizing their relationship; the pair who are clearly mated but to a person of their same sex. Are all those non-married people singles? I do not think so.

Understanding Singlehood

For our purposes singlehood has reference to the situation of unattached adulthood. Singles are adults who, for whatever reason, are not now living in a committed relationship with another adult. The opposite of single might be unsingle, with marriage being one way of becoming unsingle.

In the next chapter I shall address some of the theological

1

concerns related to singlehood, and then in the remaining chapters the care and counseling of singles. However, as a backdrop, I want to focus here on understanding singlehood. Who *are* the single adults in our midst? What are they like? What personal and interpersonal concerns characterize their lives? How do they tend to feel and think? This chapter is addressed to questions such as these. We will consider singles in terms of four major types—distinguished according to the source or cause of their singlehood.

Single by Death

I recently counseled two widows, both of whom had lost their minister-husbands by death. One was married to a seminary professor, the other to a denominational executive. Both women were younger than their husbands, but neither had given much thought to what might happen if she were to be left a widow. Neither was abnormal or unhealthy, yet neither was even minimally prepared for the barrage of identity questions and life style issues that began pummelling her the moment death came rushing towards her—sooner than the actuarial tables had predicted. In both cases their distress was perfectly natural under the circumstances, and they took some comfort in learning that fact.

We begin here with singlehood by death because it may be the least complicated form of singlehood. It may also be the easiest singlehood to acknowledge. Widows and widowers know, at least intellectually, that they are single, and they say so: "I lost my husband last January." This is not to imply that losing one's lifemate by death is anything less than an excruciating and traumatic experience, particularly if death comes unexpectedly. However, death has a final ring to it, and such finality can help render the process of separation clear and clean. "I was a married woman for as long as I can remember," a widow said to her pastor, "and now that book is closed." Once she was married; now she is single. What happened, for all its pain, is clear: death took her spouse. It is sad, but it can't be helped or changed. The new situation is an unmistakable fact, not to be reversed. Her single state is thus an honorable singlehood in terms of social attitudes and values. Everybody sympathizes.*

It is, however, the very honorableness of such singlehood that contains the seeds of unhealthy adaptation. I will discuss that possibility later in this chapter—the possibility of the bereaved remaining married to a person who has physically died! First, though, let's consider the steps toward healthy adjustment for a person who is single by death. This is especially important for pastors, who face the needs of single-by-death persons frequently in their practice of ministry. It is also important to understand this process because a similar path to recovery must be taken by persons who become single by divorce or abandonment.

Healthy Adjustment

If a friend of yours lost a spouse in an automobile accident and if, following that death, your friend was *not* upset, what would you think? You might wonder at such incredible composure. However, if the composure continued for long, you'd probably begin to wonder about your friend's emotional health. And well you might, for according to authorities in the field of death and dying it is normal to be upset when a loved one dies. The upset may not be apparent during the "shock stage," but it is there all the same. Thousands of years ago, a prophet of Israel wailed, "My anguish, my anguish! I writhe in pain! Oh, the walls of my heart!" (Jer. 4:19). Jeremiah's pain felt terminal at that moment, like life dying, but his behavior and lament were healthy and normal, given his circumstances. Every pastor has met singles who feel like Jeremiah. In the face of such grief, it is helpful to understand that strong grief feelings can be completely appropriate. It is healthy for the bereaved to experience themselves as heartsick, mentally numb, spiritually bleeding, and physically "wiped out" when they are made single by death.

Grief can be a good thing. It is surely a necessary thing. Grief work appropriately accomplished is indeed good grief.†

The term "grief" comes from a Latin word meaning "heaviness of spirit." There are many kinds of grief, but the process always involves suffering, feelings of failure and lostness, and downright anguish.

Experts have identified in healthy adults at least seven dynamics in the normal grieving process: shock, catharsis, depression, guilt, preoccupation with the loss, anger, and finally recovery. In a moment we will discuss these dynamics in greater detail. Right now I want to emphasize that the hallmark of a thorough and good grief process is adequate recovery from the loss that triggered the grief. After loss of a spouse, this process usually takes from three to five years in the healthy adult. (Pastors will be familiar with persons for whom it has taken longer.) It is for this reason that widows or widowers—or divorced persons—who quickly remarry may be marrying on the rebound, a perilous procedure.* To remarry before one's necessary grief work is complete is to bring the burden of unfinished business to a new marriage and a new mate.

To do good grieving is simply to grieve wisely and well—effectively, efficiently, and as long as necessary but no longer. I have seen a surviving spouse achieve full recovery after the death of a mate in considerably less than three years, when the mourner has done effective, efficient grieving—good grief.

Counseling Suggestions

Counselors can be helpful to that end. Here are three assignments I have given to counselees made single by death. In some instances these suggestions are made one at a time over a period of many months. In other instances, in the face of blocked grief, I have recommended all three at once.

Go Grieve

Whatever wants to happen within you, let it happen. Don't fight it; don't ignore it. Jesus wept openly at the tomb of his friend Lazarus, and Jesus was a healthy person. David grieved over the death of his soul mate Jonathan and wrote poems about it. Ruth and Naomi grieved over the loss of their husbands, and all the city knew they were grieving. The disciples grieved over the loss of Jesus at his death. Especially in the early stages of your grieving process, cry as much as possible. Once the initial shock begins to pass, tears can help a lot. Catharsis (release) is natural and normal. Let it happen. Go grieve.

Let Your Mate Go

Don't try to keep yourself tied to your spouse, or your spouse to you, in any way. As soon as you can, donate the personal wardrobe and other belongings to a charity. Once you can bear to bid farewell to the place you both called home, move away to a nest all your own. Do not avoid the pain associated with death by escaping into the home of your daughter, son, or a friend or relative. Cherish your fond memories, but don't cling to your mate as a person, or to the life you had together.

There are people whose spouses die (or divorce them) who then refuse to let go. They fear losing their identity as a husband or wife so much that long after the fact they cling steadfastly to smashed hopes and dreams in almost morbid fashion, like hanging onto a dead horse which can no longer be ridden. Pastors counseling such persons can help them ask themselves: "What are the advantages of clinging to a relationship no longer available to me?" "What are the disadvantages of letting go of the one who is gone?" There *is* a time to let go.

Think Single

To think, speak, act, and feel single takes learning, relearning, and practice. However, it must be done. The task is to provide for yourself what was formerly provided by your mate. This means taking inventory of your internal and external resources and putting them to use. It means learning to be your own best friend. The "how to" will become clearer as you grow in singlehood, *as* a single. Pastors and other counselors are there to help, but the task is yours. It is a challenge to be faced by each new single, a goal to be diligently pursued.

Bad Grief

A minister I know accepted a call to a church whose only previous pastor had served it for thirty-eight years prior to his death. Although the founding pastor had been dead for over a year and his successor was acknowledged to be winsome and competent, the relationship between the new pastor and the congregation simply did not develop. Within another year that church found itself again in search of a pastor. The problem was that the congregation had not done its grief work. Emotionally it was still "married" to its founding pastor. Bad grief is simply grief work not yet done—unresolved grief, blocked grief, disdained grief. Bad grief can lead to years, or even a lifetime, of stalemate, remaining quagmired, stuck in some stage of the grieving process and unready for rebirth and renewal.

The Dynamics of Grief

In this context we can return appropriately to the seven dynamics of the grieving process mentioned above.* Pastors called to counsel single-by-death persons might help them ascertain where they are along this seven-step path to wholeness, or at least keep the seven in mind as significant touchstones on their journey.

Shock

The shock stage is nearly always first. It is characteristic of early grief crisis. People in shock feel numb. Sometimes they speak of what is happening as "unreal," as if these events must be happening to somebody else. A man whose wife drowned said to his pastor: "The whole scene is just like watching a horror movie . . . only I'm in it!"

Catharsis

People in grief tend to go in and out of shock, catharsis, depression, and anger. However, it is appropriate to list catharsis as the stage following shock, for it is often experienced next.

Catharsis is usually defined as "the process of bringing repressed ideas and feelings into consciousness."* "Repressed" in this context simply means "held back." Catharsis is experienced, often gradually but sometimes suddenly, as a surge of feeling, a rush of emotion. There may be tears—inner tears or outer, visible tears, the latter being more effective because they are overtly released rather than suppressed.

For the widow or widower, catharsis is the venting of that which has remained pent-up during the dying and since the death of the spouse. It usually occurs, stops, and then recurs, again and again. But when the catharsis is finished, it releases the mourning person and relief is felt. Sometimes a single-by-death person feels like the crying will go on forever. It may help to say to such a person: "When you are ready, your tears will give you up."

Depression

Depression is a loaded word, because few persons want to think of themselves as depressed, but it is an accurate word. After the death of one's mate it is normal somewhere along the road to recovery to arrive at a place of acute depression. Depression usually follows after shock and catharsis, several weeks or months down the road. As with catharsis, it may come and go. Grieving people speak of fits of depression, bouts with depression, waves of depression.

Depression is the most dangerous dynamic of the grief process—a time for the pastor to pay special attention to what is happening in the life of a mourning parishioner. The dangers include lowered resistance to disease; running away from reality, perhaps by frantically escaping into one's work; and turning the depressive feelings inward on oneself. Specialists feel that unexpressed anger turned inward on oneself underlies much depression. It is during these times that people make themselves sick or even renounce their own lives. Some renounce life literally—in suicide. Others in this painful condition rush into a whirl of social activities and even remarry! A psychiatrist friend of mine likens this kind of depression to a swimmer in trouble: struggling is apt to result in drowning, whereas relaxing and allowing the body to do what is natural will result in automatic surfacing.

Remember: the depressive feelings are normal and healthy, but feeding and watering them with self-pity and self-blame is not. If a grieving parishioner seems unlikely to live through the depressive feelings or requires an inordinate amount of the pastor's attention, this is the time to invoke the help of caring laypersons who have been through similar losses, or to refer the person to outside resources for psychotherapy.

Guilt

Guilt, like depression, can come repeatedly and at various points along the way, often during times of catharsis. However, it almost always does come. I have seen it take different forms: "I feel just terrible about the way I neglected my wife. If only I'd known . . . that she'd be with me for only eight years, and then be gone." "To think that the last thing I ever said to him was nasty, just plain nasty. I don't think I'll ever forgive myself." "I know what the doctor said— that he had a heart attack. But I know what really happened: I drove him until he finally worked himself to death. More, more, more . . . big me, always wanting more!"

Whatever shape the guilt takes, it needs to be acknowledged and faced head-on in counseling the single-by-death person. It is important, however, that the pastor make a distinction between appropriate guilt and neurotic guilt.* Appropriate guilt is that sense of contrition and remorse that has a legitimate basis in reality: "I feel guilty because I am guilty; I did wrong." Neurotic guilt is the product of fear of rejection or punishment. It is not rooted in reality—other than the reality of one's own inner conflicts. It can be alleviated only by self-acceptance and self-forgiveness. Because of its source and nature, neurotic guilt usually requires depth counseling or psychotherapy. Whether or not the distinction between appropriate guilt and neurotic guilt is discussed openly with the counselee is a matter for the pastor's discretion, depending on circumstances and the nature of the counseling relationship. But it is essential that the pastor distinguish between the two types of guilt because the counseling approach is different for each.

Penny Witherspoon, a woman in her forties, was enjoying a clandestine affair with one of her colleagues. Penny's husband, aware that something was alienating him from his wife, asked her to accompany him to a marriage counselor. She refused: "Everything is all right; I just need time to get something out of my system." When her husband died suddenly of a heart attack, Penny felt an enormous burden of guilt. As she poured out her feelings to Margaret Tilson some days later, Pastor Tilson recognized that Penny's guilt was reality-based and appropriate, for she had in fact been misusing her freedom to deceive her spouse, avoid intimacy in her marriage, and violate important and authentic values in her conscience. The pastor was able lovingly but candidly to confront Penny with the appropriateness of her guilt and they literally wept together. Subsequently Penny was helped to separate her own complicity from that of her husband, who was himself a compulsive worker and overweight. Eventually Penny was able to confess her irresponsibility to God, receive God's forgiveness, and move towards reconciliation with her deceased husband and towards peace with his death.

Pastor Tilson had quite a different experience with Joe Cheney. When Joe's wife died of cancer, he insisted that he was responsible for her death despite assurances from everyone around him that he was not at fault. Margaret had previously had a good pastoral relationship with Joe and his wife, and though she and Joe met regularly for several months, she was unable to lead him to accept or forgive himself. Joe also rejected the suggestion that he see a psychotherapist: "If you can't help me, Pastor, no one can." Margaret discontinued her counseling with Joe. She said of him: "It was as if he was glorying in his guilt!"

Most often the guilt in question is not this clear. Guilty singles are neither as appropriately guilty as Penny, nor as neurotically guilty as Joe. Instead, appropriate and neurotic guilt feelings are interwoven within the same person. The important point is that single adults, especially if they are single by death or divorce, often do feel guilty, whether that guilt is rooted in reality or not. Pastors can learn how to help such persons unscramble their guilt feelings and resolve them as fully as possible. Of all possible helpers, the pastor is in the best position to help grieving persons move toward realizing forgiveness—God's forgiveness for their appropriate guilt, and forgiveness of themselves for their inappropriate neurotic guilt.

Preoccupation with the Loss

A member of a church I once served never ate a meal without setting a place for her husband, long since deceased. On Carl's empty plate Nancy placed his portrait. While dining, she carried on a one-way conversation with him. She always called herself "Mrs. Carl Smith" and many years after his death she was still wearing black. Nancy wistfully recounted the life she and Carl had had together. Friends tried again and again to help her start a new life, but she objected that "Carl wouldn't approve." Finally the friends gave up and left her to her rudderless, reclusive drifting.

This is an extreme case, of course, but many persons get caught in some less apparent state of limbo. The pastor can point out to them that there is an obvious distinction between cherishing fond memories and becoming preoccupied with one's loss. Perhaps the grieving single is suffering from guilt, a misdirected sense of loyalty, a false view of marriage as "forever," or a fear of new relationships. Used carefully, a powerful pastoral tool in such cases is the gentle granting of permission to let go—permission to separate emotionally from the spouse who has already departed physically. If this approach is used, it is important to assure the widow or widower that the pastor will be available to help face future fears:

> Pastor: As your minister and Paul's friend as well as yours, I think it's time for you to begin a new life— without Paul.
>
> Mary: You really think Paul would approve if I stopped acting like a widow?
>
> Pastor: Mary, I'd think he'd be pleased. Furthermore, I think God would also like to see you happier, and having some fun.
>
> Mary: I don't know—I have to admit I've thought about it. I guess the truth is I'm sort of scared to venture out into the world of relationships, after being married to Paul for so many years.
>
> Pastor: I appreciate your sharing that fear with me. I want you to know that once you begin that venture. I'll be glad to listen to how it's going for you, anytime, if you think that would help.
>
> Mary: Thank you. It does help to know you care.

Anger

Anger is a powerful emotion in human life.* When it appears in the grieving process, welcome it. Let's say, for example, that you have been counseling a widow for some time, and today she arrives outraged that the settling of her husband's financial affairs is dragging on and on because his will was outdated and inadequate. Find a way to congratulate her! Let her know that anger is the emotional lifeblood of the grieving person, a definite "plus sign" along the road to recovery, and a way of resolving residual depression. There comes a time for the mourner to be angry whether the reasons for the anger are clear or not. Such angry feelings are natural and normal, although they may certainly get handled in inappropriate ways. (It would be inappropriate, for example, to misdirect anger away from its real target by perhaps turning it inward and retreating into guilt or depression.) Some single-by-death persons may be angry at themselves for failing to do or say all they wanted to before that final separation. A few may be angry at their minister for being of so little help! Whatever the cause of the anger, they ought not to suppress its expression. The anger should be acknowledged and the ideas or issues which spawned it should be examined and resolved.

It may be important to help the counselee distinguish appropriate, reality-based anger from inappropriate anger, for instance anger that is a smoke screen to cover guilt or fear. A useful counseling tool is to mention some of the angry episodes recorded in the New Testament. Jesus, Peter, and Paul all manifested anger openly. Many devout people seem to identify piety with an absence of anger—which is one reason why counseling help is often needed at this point.

Recovery

There finally comes a time when one's grieving days are done; they have become past history. Humans are highly flexible beings. They have a marvelous potential to adapt. Adapting is easier for children, perhaps, but all of us have seen adults too transcend tremendous losses—loss of a child, loss of a limb, loss of eyesight, loss of a spouse after many years of marriage. Since life is not static but dynamic, always requiring adaptation to new circumstances, our future lies in our ability to recover from losses.

Acknowledging Singlehood

I have noticed in my counseling practice that when it comes to acknowledging singlehood, and feeling and acting single, widows and widowers resist more than do divorced persons and other singles. Perhaps that is because they perceive their loss as greater, deeper, or more socially acceptable. Whatever the reason, they seem to have difficulty letting go of the past and *being* single. Single-by-death persons who have trouble accepting singlehood can garner useful insights from people whose singlehood has come by other means, for singles are more similar than dissimilar in some substantial ways.

Single by Divorce

This book does not argue for divorce or against it. Its purpose rather is to promote creative singlehood after divorce occurs. I am sensitive to the biblical and church-historical injunctions pertaining to divorce. There is a constructive and theologically sound function for such injunctions, namely to affirm the biblical ideal of faithfulness to a commitment, and to challenge people not to be capricious in giving up on a relationship. Some people seek divorce when they might better realize growth by remaining in and working at their marriage; others stay married, at least in the legal sense, when their relationship is irretrievably defunct and destructive. Surely, most people do what they deem best for their preservation as persons.

It makes little, if any, difference whether a single adult happens to be the divorcer or the divorcee. I am using the term "divorcee" generically here to mean a person involuntarily divorced at his or her spouse's insistence. In most cases it is painfully difficult to be left by one's spouse. In most cases it is also painfully difficult to leave one's spouse. Of course there are variables from case to case, such as those that ensue when a person has been rejected in favor of a new lover, or when children are in the picture. The pain of the rejector may be of a different sort than that of the rejected one, but divorce always results in pain for both parties and that pain can be enormous and pervasive.

As divorcing and divorced persons bring their pain to the counseling pastor, what matters is that these hurting ones be helped to understand. They need to understand what happened in their marriages, and they need to understand what is going on within themselves.

Establishing Rapport

In order to facilitate such growth in understanding—and because the pastor is often perceived as a person who believes that divorce is sin and that marriage ought to be preserved at all costs—it can be helpful to establish counselor-counselee rapport by saying something like this: "I accept you exactly as you are, with all that has happened in your life." If as a pastor you do not *feel* that accepting, you might say what you honestly feel: "I want to listen to you, to feel with you, and to try to understand."

The important thing is for pastors to convey to the hurting person the fact of their caring and to do so in ways and words that are comfortable to both counselor and counselee. One minister said to a man at whose wedding he had officiated: "Having helped you try marriage, I'm glad you've come to me to help you try divorce." What must be conveyed is the pastor's acceptance of the counselee, tolerance of what is happening, and readiness to help the person live through it until the present potential for growth has been realized. That is the place to begin the counseling relationship—with sincere acceptance.

The Dynamics of Divorce

From this springboard it is important to discover and examine what has happened and is happening within the counselee. It may be helpful in this connection for us to ask at this point: "What do single-by-divorce persons have in common? As they become single, what growth tasks do they typically face?" All divorced people are not the same, of course, but there are some prevalent dynamics among them for which the counseling pastor can and ought to look. We can identify four major dynamics that are typical of divorced singles.

Anger

Divorced people are angry people. I have yet to meet a divorcing or recently divorced single who is not an angry person. This is readily understandable if we recall that divorce-related anger is really the person's reflexive emotional response to perceived rejection. Rejection, or perceived rejection, accompanies divorce like a wake follows the path of a ship. Rejectors reject because they fear or feel rejection. Rejectees reject because they feel a need to defend against the possibility of further rejection. Rejection itself tends to engender further rejection, and more anger.

The important point to communicate in counseling is that "It is all right to be angry." The following conversation occurred in a support group for divorced singles:

Sue: I feel so much anger, yet I know I shouldn't be angry—Tom and I had a lot of good years together. Even though I feel I just had to divorce him, I want it to be, you know, a friendly divorce.

Carol: I thought like that too, for months and months. But now that a couple of years have gone by, I know better. I feel like saying to you: "Don't even bother to dream the silly dream of a friendly divorce."

Pastor: It would probably make more sense if you dreamed that your ex got run over by a steam roller. A couple have a friendly divorce only if there was no intensity of relationship in the first place—in which case I would question whether they really had a marriage. [Pause] Divorce is not amicable, or civilized, or logical. Divorce is an ordeal—an unwanted, untimely, crazy death.

Sue: I'm beginning to see what you mean.

Pastor: What interests me, Sue, is how are you doing with your anger? (At this point the counselor was able to help the group talk about ways to deal with anger in a healthy manner.)*

Crisis

Divorced people are people in crisis. In saying that single-by-divorce persons are in crisis, I am implying two things: First, divorce in and of itself tends to precipitate a crisis even in the healthiest of adults—those who ordinarily take life's exigencies in stride. Second, the weeks, months, and even years following marital dissolution may render divorced persons more prone to additional crises—traffic tickets, career upheaval, overextending themselves financially—than they would have been under less stressful circumstances. Thus, the pastoral counselor does well to inquire about personal problems and how the counselee is handling them.*

The Chinese word for "crisis" consists of two characters, the first signifying "danger" and the second "opportunity." Crises are indeed "dangerous opportunities," and thus it is not surprising when pastors find that some divorced persons grow in wisdom and maturity through the experience while others seem to flounder in and out of one crisis after another.

A crisis may be defined as a person's internal reaction to an external event of an emotionally hazardous nature. The emotionally hazardous events which trigger crises are most often interpersonal in nature, and a key word in understanding crisis dynamics is the word "loss." Note the clarity of this theme in the following exchange:

Pastor: So Jane and the children have moved to Kansas.
Phil: Yes, just as I had feared they would. I feel completely lost without them.
Pastor: That helps me understand why you seem so low.
Phil: Not just low—lost. I guess I'm just a loser.
Pastor: You've sustained a gigantic loss, but you are certainly not a loser.
Phil: I feel like one. Everything I had is gone.

Does this sound familiar? Phil is experiencing crisis, a time of emotional imbalance, spiritual disequilibrium, psychological vulnerability, and "dangerous opportunity."

As in the face of anger, it is important for the counselor to project a positive attitude in confronting crisis: "It is good that you have come to me in your time of crisis." Crisis is a normal state of emotional affairs, and the counselor must not attempt to talk the client out of experiencing it. As we shall see in chapter 3, counselors need to acknowledge the presence of crisis, the unwelcome intruder, and then walk through that distressing valley with the client.

Grief

Divorced people are grieving people. Marital separation usually precedes divorce, but separation is not the same as divorce. Even when *de jure* divorce, divorce in the legal sense, is over, emotional divorce may have occurred only partially if at all. The feelings one experiences preceding the dissolution of a relationship are anticipatory; they never match those attending the final blow. One must still grieve *after* the actual loss has occurred. Since the dynamics of grief in the divorced are similar to those of the single-by-death person, the counselor's task is again that of a grief facilitator.

In their grief some divorced singles feel as if they embody every emotional "illness" a person could possibly contract. Often they are additionally distressed or depressed over feeling this way. It can help to point out to them that feeling sick or "crazy in the head" is common among the divorced. From a counseling perspective feelings of that sort can also be put to productive use. In the church of my childhood I remember the visiting evangelist exhorting the crowd: "You want to be saved? First you'd better admit you are lost!" He may have made his point crudely, but he did have a point: an indispensable prerequisite to transcending one's condition is to know there is a condition to transcend.

It also helps to be able to articulate what that condition is. Most divorced singles not only know they are feeling bad; they also have some ideas about why they are feeling as they do. Often they are feeling a sense of grievous loss or "grievously lost." With a bit of encouragement from their counselor they can clarify their feelings and put them into words— "loss" or "lost" are the words to listen for.

To put the point another way: marriage is usually a disappointing experience. This is because the expectations most people bring to marriage are to some degree exaggerated and unrealistic. Divorce is an even more disappointing experience, and disappointment is a much underrated emotion. It hurts, it embarrasses, it upsets one's sense of balance and purpose. The sense of loss that comes with divorce is awful. Thus it is all right to grieve. In fact grief is altogether appropriate, for there is much reason to grieve.

You will recall that in the normal grief process of healthy adults, full recovery after the death of a spouse or after other significant loss often takes from three to five years. In singlehood by divorce, along with the loss of an all-important relationship there may be additional emotional hurdles to overcome. Therefore the grief work attendant upon divorce can sometimes be more complicated than that following bereavement. For instance, some divorced singles feel a deep sense of personal failure, like the woman who kept repeating: "No one has ever been divorced in my family—not on my mother's side, not on my father's side—no one ever, as far back as we can trace our roots, until me. I had to be the one to blow it." Other divorced singles experience setbacks in their grief process because ex-spouses or children, who have their own agendas and needs, are less than cooperative. Still others find their pain exacerbated by the pain in their family of origin. Jerry, a man in his thirties whose wife had left him to follow her professional career goals, was already in a state of acute depression when his mother phoned to tell him: "My total sympathy is with Angie. I told her before she married you that you'd be no prize. I don't see how anyone could ever live with you." Difficulties and cruelties such as these can slow down or stultify the grief process—which is one reason why a caring pastoral relationship can be invaluable to the life of a divorced single.

Dependency

Divorced people are dependent people. To be human, of course, is to be dependent. Dependency is that trait within each of us whereby we insist on receiving confirmation of our worth from others. This need is, in and of itself, natural and healthy. However, normal dependency often becomes radically intensified under the stress of divorce. One of my counselees, during her postdivorce adjustment period, wrote:

> I've always known I was needful, but now I feel super-needful. I've been a mite off balance before, but now I'm mightily imbalanced. I used to occasionally get pangs of skin hunger, but these days my whole body longingly cries to be held. My self-esteem periodically got shaky, but now it has fallen flat on its proverbial face. Worst of all, my confidence in my ability to select appropriate people as soul friends was at an all-time high when I trusted myself to Jack to be his wife "till death do us part," but right now I wouldn't trust myself to pick an edible piece of fruit out of a whole orchard full of ripe peaches.

Because I had known the writer well and she now lived in a distant city, I felt drawn to answer her letter, in part, as follows:

> I think it good that you are so closely in touch with your dependency needs. You seem wiser and in a good position to learn about all of your inner dynamics—to understand them, own them, respect their power, flow with them, and even embrace them. If you can do so, I think there will come some joy one day—maybe even pretty soon. To help you, I'd suggest that you try to find a support group with whom you can share your journey. Why not seek out a group of women in the church you attend or in the university community?

Within a few months I received another letter. My friend had found a support group; her crisis was past and she had come to a place of calm in her singlehood.

Single by Default

Other terms might seem innocuous by comparison—deferment, delay, postponement, inaction. The world of the never married and formerly married, however, is populated with many who in their own estimation are single by "default," in the simple dictionary meanings of that word: "failure to act; neglect; want; lack; absence."* These are people who view marriage as normative, or even as the only decent way to live. They are waiting for fate, or God, to present to them their destined mate. They see their singlehood as merely a prelude, interlude, or postlude to real living; the concert itself is for *un*singles. They think of themselves as those who have been temporarily overlooked, or have failed to show up in the right place at the right time, or are doomed to an endless wait for their ship to come in so that their singlehood can end.

A single man in his late twenties asked his pastor: "If marriage is ordained by God, why have I been kept waiting so long?" The minister replied: "Marriage may be God's will for some, but not for everybody. It could be that you aren't ready for marriage; or maybe you've expected God to drop a mate into your lap without you doing your part; or perhaps being married isn't the best way for you to live." The young adult, who did not like his pastor's response, was single by default.

I do not mean to judge this group of singles. But to become unsingle, a person has to make something happen, or at least follow the path of least resistance, least cultural pressure. Furthermore it is considered normal in Western civilized cultures for a person to wait "until the right one comes along," and then—only then—to marry. Few people would dispute the untold suffering connected with marrying too soon or marrying the wrong person. Almost everyone would agree that it is better not to marry than to endure the pain of so grave an error in timing and judgment—everyone, that is, except certain people who find themselves interminably and annoyingly single by the fateful circumstance of "default."

When I was a child in an immigrant neighborhood in Detroit, I remember asking my mother and grandmother about certain obviously mature adults in our community who were unmarried, some of whom were, of course, widows or widowers. This was viewed as "too bad," especially if they were women whose husbands had been killed in the war or women who were now, alas, too old or too poor or too unattractive ever to marry. Others, I was told, had simply never married. They had "waited too long," or "Mr. Right never came along," or "She couldn't find anyone who wanted to marry her," or even "Her trouble is she's always been too fussy." These were the pat answers if the question was about a woman. If the question was about a man, the responses were apt to be even more stereotyped: any never-married adult male was "an old bachelor," "too set in his ways"—peculiar beyond belief and probably the victim of habits so strange as to be unmentionable. In any case, I was to steer clear of him. The absolute assumption thirty years ago seemed to be that no one ever *chose* to remain single as an adult. Religious celibacy might have been the exception, but even priests and nuns and missionaries who remained single were thought to have given up the holy calling of marriage for the sake of another call to serve God and humankind. In fact, in the church I attended as a youth—when women were not yet being ordained—it was publicly stated that the reason so many single women became missionaries was because the men destined to be their husbands had refused to hear and heed the call of God!

Now, thirty years later, living in an age that has been called the post-Christian era and following the sexual revolution, we have all witnessed personally and through the media the impact of many important movements for freedom—among blacks, Hispanics, women, gays, children, and old people. We have probably wondered about the degree, depth, and durability of the changes these movements have brought, though undeniably and irrevocably they have brought *some* change. At least most of us try to avoid stereotyping and labeling people anymore—except when describing singles! Even today few people in this supposedly enlightened age talk or act as if singlehood is anything but a precursor of marriage (or of living together)—a less-than-normal condition to be characterized not in terms of what it is but in terms of what it lacks, a significant absence.

Society today includes as many single adults as there are married couples; that is, one of every three adults is nonmarried.* Most of us are aware of the high divorce rates and the increasingly numerous unhappy marriages. Still, the unspoken, unwritten assumption for most of us, old and young, straight and gay, married and nonmarried, seems to be that singlehood is a *temporary* condition. It is a condition of making do until the right person comes along and that better situation can be realized. Single people persist in telling themselves that the real way to live is, of course, in a relationship— preferably a marriage relationship, but at least in some kind of committed relationship. Sooner or later, most singles become unsingle; but many of those who remain single are single by default, because they have believed a dominant fable in our culture: "Even a bad love is better than no love at all."

Single by Choice

It is not only tolerable to be single. It is acceptable. It is all right. It can even be good! Singleness is a legitimate choice, for the long run as well as the short. It is not necessarily a better choice than being unsingle, or married; but neither is it necessarily worse. The married state can be wonderfully fulfilling; so can the nonmarried state. Spousehood can be hellish; so can singlehood. Frankly, it may be easier to create a good singlehood than a good marriage, even in a culture that regards marriage as the better way to live. This is because it is easier to grow toward wholeness as an individual than to grow toward a mature relationship requiring two whole individuals. Individuals with mutually satisfying marriages, then, have either carried a healthy singlehood into their marriage relationships, or have painstakingly developed their capacity for a high level of autonomy within their marriages. In either instance, they did not marry in hopes of curing the pain of singlehood.

The remainder of this book sets forth some attitudes and approaches that can help bring about a creative singlehood. Its emphases and data are drawn from the life experiences of a variety of single pilgrims making their way along the road to wholeness. Who can better illumine the pathway?

2. Toward a Theology of Singlehood

This book is dedicated chiefly to practical matters such as the nature of singlehood and how to minister to single adults. For the reader who participates in a theological tradition, however, I want to share some theological concerns as a context for these considerations. It is not my purpose here to propose a separate, systematic, or comprehensive theology of singlehood, but only to set down some theological ideas that are pertinent to the survival and growth of people who are single.

Singlehood and the Bible

In theologizing about singlehood, there is a paucity of direct biblical help. Jesus certainly presents a model of creative singlehood, and he was single by choice. However, Jesus had unique reasons for being single, given his messianic task. Besides, he had already completed his ministry by the time he reached his early thirties. Today, many persons older than that are just becoming single, or are embarking on a whole new career, or are wrestling with the question of whether or not to have children—in midlife! Whether the Bible student today looks at the lives of prophets, apostles, widows, harlots, or virgins—or Jesus—it is difficult for a modern single to identify with biblical "singles." As the historical document it is, the Bible remains basically patriarchal and tribal, with marriage and family regarded as normative for perpetuating the bloodline. When nonmarriage is mentioned or implied, it appears as an aberration connected with some special purpose, such as a dangerous or all-encompassing calling like that of Jesus.

Therefore, a theology that can undergird singlehood as a legitimate option for the contemporary Christian adult calls for the extrapolation of biblical principles. As in theologizing about racial equality or equality of the sexes, biblical literalism or proof-texting will not do.

A biblical principle relevant to singlehood may be inferred from one of Jesus' more peculiar sayings:

> Do not think that I have come to bring peace on earth; I have not come to bring peace, but a sword. For I have come to set a man against his father, and a daughter against her mother, and a daughter-in-law against her mother-in-law; and a man's foes will be those of his own household. He who loves father or mother more than me is not worthy of me; and he who loves son or daughter more than me is not worthy of me; and he who does not take his cross and follow me is not worthy of me. He who finds his life will lose it, and he who loses his life for my sake will find it.
>
> —Matt. 10:34–39

I do not think Jesus is here speaking out against the family, although he may be reminding his followers that he did not come to earth to guarantee them comfort and peace and a happy life. What is being said, in the context of the passage and of Matthew's Gospel, is this: Sometimes, if you are faithful to yourself and to your mission in life as a Christian, you will pay a price. You may need to choose between living the truth and keeping the peace. You may reap trouble and dissension even in your own family, if you break from their tradition. Thus, even on the home front you may be forced to choose between a "fake peace" purchased at the price of faithfulness and a commitment that leads to a solitary journey into the unknown.

Many Christian people who idolize marriage view singlehood with condescension. Implicitly they regard marriage and childbearing as the will of God for every human being. Whoever chooses singlehood may thus be seen as "stepping right out of the will of God," as one mother put it to her daughter—

and that is anathema. In some cases I have seen singlehood alienate single adults from their parents and other kinfolk. In other words, choosing to be single can leave one feeling very much alone.

Aloneness

According to the dictionary, a main meaning of single is "lone," and the term "single" is offered as a primary synonym for the word "alone."* It is a thesis of this book that creative singlehood has to do with creative aloneness, and since aloneness is vital to singlehood a definition of aloneness may be helpful at this point.

"Aloneness" means not only separate, apart, or isolated from others, but also unique, unequaled, or even unexcelled, as in the sentence: "She is alone among her peers in devotion to her career." "Loneliness" is virtually identical to aloneness, although in a heightened sense "loneliness" may also connote without company or companionless. Loneliness may be thought of as the feeling dimension of aloneness, since aloneness simply connotes a state of being. Certainly to many single adults loneliness seems inextricably interwoven into the fabric of aloneness. In any case, aloneness and loneliness are virtually inseparable, although a person can be creatively single and alone without consistently choosing to be without company or companionless.

The important idea here is that aloneness and loneliness can be positive and useful. They are best viewed in contrast to lonesomeness, which cannot be positive. Lonesomeness clearly points to a depressed feeling of being alone, a sad or disquieting feeling of isolation; it connotes a *longing* for companionship. I have known depressing lonesomeness. I have also seen its devastating effects on many people. A physician of my acquaintance, having been married and divorced several times, told me that he had never conquered a lifelong battle with lonesomeness. At night, he confessed, he would cry himself to sleep and often drink himself to sleep. Sadly, he has since been married and divorced yet another time.

In creative singlehood, lonesomeness is to be transcended. This is accomplished by learning how to handle aloneness, and companionlessness or loneliness as necessary. It is my hope that this book will help both pastoral counselors and single adults with that task.

Singlehood and Aloneness

To me, thinking theologically about singlehood means, most of all, thinking about aloneness. During my years as a single adult I found myself wrestling a lot with the notions of the meaning of existence and of life. I am anything but a thorough-going existentialist; arguments about whether existence precedes essence or vice versa have always exasperated or bored me. However, I think there are some existentialist ideas with which singles ought to reckon. One is that in a very real sense each of us is born alone, lives alone, and dies alone. The Old Testament writer put it succinctly: "Naked I came from my mother's womb, and naked shall I return" (Job 1:21).

For several years as a hospital chaplain I called on dying people. Gradually I learned some ways to be present by their bedside with comfort and even cheer. Often, they came to view me as a representative of God. But when the moment of death arrived, I saw them die alone. True, having a caring person to hold their hand seemed to make a difference in their dying. I also exulted in the difference a vital faith made; I saw that God, experienced as real and really "there," could truly transmute pain and angst, anxious dread of the unknown. But this does not alter the fact that each of us dies alone. Jesus too died alone. No one can die with another, or for another. Even when surrounded by a circle of loving people, each person faces death alone. Coming to grips with this fact can be helpful to a single adult. I have known several singles who, according to their own statements, actually married so they wouldn't have to die alone. If their marriages last and they predecease their mates, their spouses may indeed help them in their dying processes; but at the end they still must die alone.

Not only does one face death alone; one also lives life

alone. Even when life is enriched by many opportunities to be a lover, playmate, parent, or trusted friend, each individual is alone. There is simply a pervasive aloneness about life. Women have reported feeling it during pregnancy, even when they felt "copregnant" with a loving husband. When we sleep each night, we do so with only the inner company of our own dreams, and we remain alone until called back into wakeful consciousness. Thus each of us had best learn to sleep alone— tolerably, peaceably, even joyously. Many people have married because they couldn't tolerate sleeping by themselves. What they may have failed to recognize is that: ". . . great marriages cannot be constructed by individuals who are terrified by their basic aloneness, as so commonly is the case, and seek a merging in marriage. Genuine love not only respects the individuality of the other but actually seeks to cultivate it, even at the risk of separation or loss. The ultimate goal of life remains the spiritual growth of the individual, the solitary journey to peaks that can be climbed only alone."*

The question is: how does the single who is in fact alone make peace with that aloneness?

I must admit that I have never yet mastered aloneness for any prolonged period. I'm not sure that protracted aloneness is possible or desirable for most people. Jesus openly showed his need for companionship and intimacy, but some people, like Jesus, seem to be much more skilled than others at being alone. I am grateful that through my single years I grew considerably in my own self-support skills, including my relative ability to be alone and to live alone with equanimity. But even if perfect acceptance of aloneness remains more an ideal than a reality, commitment to its value and learning as much as possible about it are keys to creative singlehood.

The way to become expert at aloneness is not through discounting togetherness. On the contrary, creative aloneness demands that one recognize the value of togetherness. No one who has ever been "in love"† could fail to pay homage to Aphrodite, the goddess of love. Nevertheless, for the confessing Christian—and I speak as one—Jesus is Lord. This means that Jesus is the Lord of Aphrodite as he is the Lord of Mars (the god of courage and honor), of Athena (the goddess of wisdom and art), and of Jupiter (the god of power and strength). Though these gods and goddesses have symbolic value, by his death and resurrection Jesus put them to the test and they were found inadequate.

For the single Christian, then, it is not romantic love and romantic togetherness (whether real or an "illusion of fusion") that enables creative living. For example, romantic love never enables one to love the unlovable in oneself, the ugliness we all have in us. For Christians who acknowledge his lordship, Jesus does seem to enable this quality of love in their lives, this self-acceptance. Perhaps Jesus' spirit can do such enabling today precisely because Jesus was so skilled at being single and alone. According to the New Testament writers, Jesus spent much time and energy in being alone, and he was apparently competent at it.

To be alone and to master that aloneness is an enormous task. It is the task of learning to know yourself, love yourself, have mercy on yourself, be kind and gentle to yourself, laugh at yourself, forgive yourself, unsentimentalize your view of yourself, and be more and more self-supporting. In short, it is learning to be your own best friend. One can be *well-married to oneself*. This is perhaps the main message the pastoral counselor has for single adults: unless at some time and in some place in our lives we are alone, and experience that aloneness (and loneliness) for what it is, unless we learn to be creative with it, and integrative with it, we humans have relatively little to bring to other persons when we do love them. Instead all we bring them is our own needs, demands, passions, fears, jealousies, and well-intentioned but conflicted gestures. Wise singles will beware of the seductiveness of those needy persons who treat themselves like refuse while imploring others to treat them like diamonds.

Celebrating Aloneness

The most helpful first step in consciousness-raising along the path to mastering aloneness is for each of us to discover individually the naked beauty of who we are. It is for each of us to celebrate our child-of-Godness, our womanness, our manness, our blackness, our whiteness, our elderliness, our youthfulness—just who and what God intended when God made us. To do this is first to face and celebrate the fact that we are alone—which means also to celebrate the fact that we are free. When we actually lay claim to being alone and free, it seems to have an explosive effect.

I once witnessed the mystery and truth of just such an explosion in an ecumenical singles group. Singles of diverse colors, ages, and life styles were present and all seemed to feel at home. I noted that there was no pressure to conform to any prescribed criteria; there were no rules for membership. The theological premise of the group was clearly conveyed: In this organization there is neither Jew nor Gentile, there is neither poor nor rich, there is neither blue collar nor white collar, there is neither male nor female, there is neither gay nor straight, there is neither old nor young. None of these things matter, for we are all one in Christ. The only attributes we hold in common are that we are single and children of God.*

Liberation movements can ultimately help liberate everyone, not merely the people who are direct beneficiaries. Thus black liberation can help liberate white people as well as blacks; women's liberation can help liberate men as well as women; gray liberation can help liberate the young as well as their elders; and gay liberation can also help liberate heterosexuals. When Jesus said, "You will know the truth, and the truth will make you free" (John 8:32), he was correctly implying that truth, when brought into the open, always frees.

It never hurts to remind ourselves that while anyone is in bondage, we all are in bondage. If I treat a woman as a nonperson, as a stereotype, I too become a stereotype—a stereotypical chauvinist—because I am dealing in falsehood. If I treat a single as a nonperson, as a stereotype—unfulfilled because nonmarried—once again I become a stereotype myself because I am dealing in falsehood. I have been guilty of such stereotyping, and I have known male pastors who tended to stereotype both women and single adults. When a woman refuses to let me treat her as a stereotype, she may be opening the door for me to become liberated from my false posture. So also with persons who are alone: when singles refuse to let me stereotype them, they help me become freer. In this sense celebrating aloneness can be a freeing thing for everyone. It can mean fruitful confrontation of ministers who have been less than egalitarian toward all people. It can be a liberating force for churches that have oriented themselves only to married couples and families while neglecting or ignoring singles.

Furthermore, celebrating aloneness can help free people who are married or living in other committed relationships. Just as there is a black within each of us, and a woman and a child and an elder (who can be liberated by the liberation of their group), so there is also an aloneness within even the most idyllic relationship that can be freed when those who live singly and alone celebrate their aloneness. Thus I harbor the dream that singles will help raise the consciousness of all of us in this regard, will help free us. Then husbands will perhaps feel less guilty when they need to be alone. Wives will perhaps more freely assert their need for time alone and space apart in their lives. Lovers can perhaps let their lovers have thoughts and dreams and fantasies that are not violated by constant probing, nagging, and interrogating.

Part of that dream involves a homily, a brief sermon that in fantasy I dream of delivering to singles:

> Single adults, rest in the thought that God is present to meet you just where you are, and to help you celebrate exactly what is happening right now in your singlehood. That is the incredible message of the gospel. "Do not say 'lo here' or 'lo there' is the kingdom of God," Jesus said, "for the kingdom of God is within you" [Luke 17:20–21]. "Within me?" you may ask. "In my apartment alone watching television? Looking in the mirror and seeing only myself?" Yes. Those singles who hope for a knight in shining armor or a fairy-tale princess to bring them that new consciousness and caring which is "the kingdom" are merely avoiding having to face finding

God in the earthy stuff of their own everyday existence, in the here and now.

Think of God as the One who opens your eyes to see clearly the vitality, joy, and pain of life as it is—exactly there where you are right now. Then, with eyes wide open, you can change, grow, move on, meet people, love people, marry or not marry, have relationships or not. You can do whatever seems to make for harmony and freedom in your life.

It is possible, of course, to make another kind of choice. You can choose to avoid yourself, even despise yourself, and count your aloneness as some kind of curse to escape; but then you will be denying the very fabric of the gospel. Jesus was a single adult who demonstrated ultimate freedom in his living, dying, and rising alone. Jesus' freedom is God's gift to the single person of our day. And that freedom is more readily available now than ever before because we live in a highly pluralistic society, a society in which one is quite free to choose how one will live in God's sight.

Jesus modeled the freedom to resist societal pressures to conform to what the dominant culture says one must do in order to enjoy a satisfying life. One of Jesus' apostles put it this way: "Don't let the world around you squeeze you into its own mold, but let God remold your minds from within, so that you may prove in practice that the plan of God for you is good . . . and moves toward the goal of true maturity." [Rom. 12:2, Phillips translation].

Singlehood can be an okay way to live, but it can also be far more than that—it can be a righteous way to live.

3. Singlehood and Survival

Greg Walker phoned his pastor in the middle of the night: "Reverend Jones, I hate to bother you but . . . [sobbing] . . . I just don't think I'm going to make it. I've been crying all night. I can't sleep. I can't even eat."

Howard Jones thought quickly. "Can you meet me at eight o'clock in the coffee shop across from the church?"

"Yes, I'll be there."

"Good. Try to get some rest now and I'll see you at eight."

Greg was a handsome, athletic, thirty-five-year-old deacon in the church. He had a good education and a high-paying job. Why, wondered the pastor, was he so distraught? Then Howard remembered: the woman who had been accompanying Greg to church was missing last Sunday—Greg had sat alone. Could that be it?

It was. At breakfast Greg told the pastor that he had asked Dottie to marry him and that her response had been to break off the relationship. Recently divorced, Greg was having difficulty surviving on his own. He was desperately seeking a new Mrs. Walker. The pastor and Greg agreed to meet regularly for the next six weeks to talk about some ways for Greg to survive without getting married.

This chapter deals with survival skills for singles. It envisions growth toward a holistic singlehood, a movement towards wellness in the major aspects of their everyday living as single adults. I make no claim to being comprehensive; for example, I have left such subjects as physical health and money management* to other authors. Still, certain basic learnings seem crucial for sheer survival as a single adult. These aspects

of single living have not only surfaced repeatedly in my counseling relationships with singles; they have also been of great
moment in my personal journey as a single adult. I will approach each topic as a pastor-counselor, speaking to both the
single person's need and the counselor's task.

Living Alone

One of the problems singles encounter when faced with the
possibility of living alone is summed up in the memorable line
of a comic strip character, Walt Kelly's Pogo: "We has met
the enemy and they is us." A minister reported the following
conversation:

> Merri: Hal has asked to move in with me and I'm thinking
> about letting him.
>
> Pastor: The last time we talked you said you were starting
> to feel okay about living alone.
>
> Merri: I thought I was. But then Hal came along and . . .
> well, it isn't natural to live all by yourself, is it? You
> know, birds of a feather and all that.
>
> Pastor: I'm wondering about your feelings for Hal.
>
> Merri: Oh, I don't love him or anything like that, if that's
> what you mean. We've agreed not to have sex or any-
> thing. He'd just be like, you know, a housemate, or a
> companion. After all, it's a shame to be in that big old
> house all by myself. [Pause] Even economically, it's a
> waste, and ecologically, too.
>
> Pastor: That's probably true. But in this instance the greater
> shame or waste could be Merri's not utilizing this time
> for an opportunity to live alone.

There are reasons why singles like Merri find it difficult
to live alone for any protracted period. The first is, as Pogo's
line implied, that people undermine themselves. A nonmarried man put it this way during a counseling session: "I've
become so brainwashed that I honestly feel there's something
wrong with me for liking my own company so well. I actually
feel selfish or tainted for so thoroughly enjoying a sunset or a

symphony, alone. It's like I'm always looking back over my own shoulder and wondering: ought not I to be sharing this with someone?" Singles frequently sabotage themselves when it comes to enjoying their singlehood.

A second difficulty, of course, is the enormous impact of the culture which surrounds us. Note the words of the same counselee later during the same interview:

> The other morning I woke up feeling good, at peace with myself. I was alone and happy. I enjoyed my coffee and the morning news. I left for work calm, cool, and collected. By the end of the day I felt so bombarded by the togetherness messages on billboards, radio, and TV—images of everybody doing everything in groups of two or more—that I came back home lonely. Well, not genuinely lonely; more like lonely because I thought I was *supposed* to feel lonely. I was thinking: if I'm not lonely, what's wrong with me?

The world in which we live will disturb the peace of singles, if the singles allow it.

Third, many if not most singles are addicted to the notion of romantic love. Such addiction is not new; it is an idolatry that has plagued humankind for several centuries. Up to the thirteenth century or so, the notion of romantic love was left mostly to poets and bards. People got married or they didn't, but if they did it was for economic, religious, and procreative reasons. Typically, love became part of a relationship only later if at all. In any case, love was not the romanticized mystery we moderns tend to make of it. It was simply a part of the earthiness of human relationships. For some, perhaps for the rich, it may have been just a luxury to dally in, but in no way necessary to the business of everyday living. It is only during the past several centuries, then, that love in its sentimentalized form has come to be seen as *the* necessity for "normal" living. It is as if the poetic utterances of the troubadours, then and now, have been canonized as a norm.

So, as sophisticated, intelligent, and wise as the singles of today may be, many of them still believe devoutly and hope fervently that some day, somehow, Mr. or Miss or Ms. Right will come along and lift their burden of lonesomeness, turn their night into day, fill their eyes with tears of joy and their ears with whispers of sweet nothings, create instant passion day or night, and with peace and comfort lead them hand in hand into paradise. If the point seems melodramatic, I have made it so on purpose because this is how many if not most single adults actually feel, for all their facade of street-wise worldliness.

Living alone, of course, is not the only choice single adults can make. It is one choice among others—and a good one. It can help singles learn new and important ways of using their freedom to make choices, wholesome choices about how to live and with (or without) whom. Indeed the most important prerequisite for being well-married to another person is to be first *well-married to oneself,* and one good way to achieve that state of personal wellness is through the learnings that accompany living alone. A time of singlehood can often be the best time—even the only time—to try living alone. Because this is so, pastoral counselors should encourage single clients to give serious consideration to this option. I strongly favor this option because of the invaluable learnings I derived from the experience of living alone between my first marriage and my present one. However, the growth experience of learning to be well-married to oneself is *not* something to be sought only as preparation for marriage! It is also a key to being creatively single for life on an ongoing basis, indeed for being a whole person.

Handling Crises

As we have seen, single-by-divorce persons are sometimes crisis-prone. For this reason crisis management is an important survival skill for singles to learn. Indeed they need that skill, whether divorced or not, because of their heightened vulnerability to crises. The dilemma Marjorie faced suggests the wide-ranging character of their vulnerability:

> First I was told that I should reciprocate for a nice first date by speaking up and asking the man for the second date, without waiting for him to ask me; I tried that twice, and both times the men assumed that my invitation meant the second date would naturally end in bed. Then I was told to be asser-

tive and not wait around for an invitation but come right out and ask whomever I wanted for a date; I tried that three times and all three men flatly rejected my overture. Now I'm in a worse emotional state than I was before when I wasn't trying to date at all.

The single person is no stranger to events that precipitate crises.

Singles need to learn workable ways of being self-reliant and self-supporting. They need to be able to handle the "dangerous opportunities" that confront them if their singlehood is to be a constructive experience. In any particular crisis the danger involved is likely to loom larger than the opportunity it may contain. For this reason the counseling pastor may wish to focus on helping the counselee see clearly the opportunity inherent in the crisis.

As we have seen, a crisis is simply a person's internal reaction to an external event of an emotionally hazardous nature. It is a time of stress and distress within. Crisis is a matter of emotional imbalance, psychological vulnerability, spiritual disequilibrium. Most often it involves either a threat of loss or an actual loss that arouses anxiety, grief, guilt, anger, depression, or even "craziness."

Jill: I can't believe what is happening to me . . . me of all people. I'm a nurse, for heaven's sake. I pride myself in being shock-proof, being able to take everything in stride. But ever since Gene left I don't know whether I'm afoot or on horseback! I find myself doing the silliest things. Yesterday I locked my keys in the trunk at the grocery store. I had to borrow a dime to call a locksmith before I could drive my own car to my own house with a trunk full of melted ice cream.

Pastor: It sounds like you're upsetting yourself over losing Gene. (Although this response to Jane was theoretically accurate in that people do upset themselves and must be responsible for their own upsets, it articulated a confrontation that was probably premature. Less intrusive and more open-ended would have been something like: "You've felt topsy-turvy lately.")

Crisis means disorientation and the person in crisis needs help to see that, yet not be thrown by it.

In addition to experiencing loss and disorientation, people in crisis face an identity problem—in Jill's case "Who am I now that Gene is gone?"—an identity problem that might otherwise have remained hidden. Herein lies the "opportunity" inherent in a crisis. This is why crises, though painful, can be used to face one's "Who am I?" dilemmas and in so doing enhance self-awareness and growth toward a fuller maturity.

Because of the pain provoked by the crisis, however, sufferers usually find it difficult to look at themselves clearly. Understandably they find it easier to run from where they are and retreat to some familiar place of safety. We are all prone to cling to our old dreams and favorite behaviors. We would rather avoid having to face the new identity which wants to emerge in and through a crisis. This is where the pastoral counselor can be of service.

> Jill: One of my friends, another doctor's wife, called me last week to invite me to a social gathering. She obviously hadn't heard about Gene and me. When I told her she seemed shocked. It was almost funny. She called me a "poor dear" and asked what in the world I was going to do. I said something about reactivating my nursing career and she said, "Now isn't that something. I've known you for years and never knew you used to be a nurse." To her, I guess I was just a big-shot surgeon's wife.
>
> Pastor: I wonder how it feels for you to give up the identity of Mrs. Well-known Physician.
>
> Jill: [Long pause] To tell you the truth, not too good.
>
> Pastor: I'd like you to think about the disadvantages of giving up that identity, and also any advantages you can think of.

Jill's counselor, it might be mentioned, was a female pastor, and that was fortunate. Surely a male can also counsel skillfully, but there are dangers when a male pastor works in a counseling capacity with a divorcing woman like Jill. The dangers include his not seeing her crisis from a woman's point of view or his being tempted to "rescue" her from the pain she is experiencing, and the possibility of sexual feelings or responses—on the part of the client or counselor, or both—hampering the counseling relationship.

A major loss, such as the loss of a mate, must be understood as involving not only the loss of an important person or relationship, but also the loss of a significant part of one's old identity and dreams. This understanding, once it is grasped, serves to modify one's upset feelings with at least the dim awareness that a new identity can be born out of the ashes of the old. To put it another way, if a crisis is to serve its best purpose the sufferer must see in it an opportunity to shed the cocoon and learn to fly. Given our human tendency to be creatures of habit, this is often a scary prospect, and therein lies the danger in a crisis. If people in crisis turn their fear into resistance, they lose the opportunity to move on to the next step in their becoming. If, on the other hand, they can be helped to face the danger, they can perhaps find courage to rise above their fear and cooperate with that inner force—God—which is trying to lead them toward a new consciousness, thus allowing the crisis to perform its best function.

> Pastor: Jill, in observing you for several years, it has seemed to me that you've always been busy; yet you've not looked happy.
>
> Jill: You're so right. Actually, I've been bored and restless, especially since our youngest daughter entered kindergarten. I've thought a lot about working outside the home again, but Gene never could understand why I'd want to do that when most of the money I'd make would go for taxes. Besides, I think he's always prided himself on supporting his family without his wife having to work.
>
> Pastor: Maybe that life style reached the limits of its value for you some time ago.
>
> Jill: Yes. I think it did when all three of our girls got to be

school age . . . though even earlier than that I can remember dreaming about working in a hospital or a med-
ical office.

Pastor: To look at things as positively as possible, now
could be an advantageous time for you to do something
about that dream.

In many cases a crisis seems to arise when a person holds
onto something old just at the point where something new
wants to emerge. Counselors do well to keep this in mind
while tenderly remembering too that crisis is a time when the
devices people have habitually used for dealing with exigencies are beginning to fail them, and people are feeling insecure
and hypersensitive. Often people need counseling help precisely because they are being thrown back on their own resources when they do not know what those resources are or
how to use them.

Jill: I don't know . . . I've gotten soft and heavier than I've
ever been, and I'm not twenty-five anymore. I'm not sure
I could stand being on my feet all day. To make matters
worse, I'm no longer sure that nursing is what I really
want to do. It's what my parents wanted me to do.

Pastor: If you could be back in school, what would you like
to study?

Jill: I don't know. [Pause] I really have no idea. [Long
pause] I'm sorry to be so scattered. It's just that I feel so
lost inside . . . like a sheep without a shepherd . . .
[Tears].

Even in the presence of her pastoral shepherd, Jill feels lost
and alone. Somehow in her solitude, and with her pastor's
help, she must discover something within herself before she
can move confidently to establish new goals and relationships.
She is not ready for strong challenges right now. Thus an
appropriate counseling response at this point might be: "Jill,
I think you are just where you need to be right now, even
though struggling with your feelings is very painful."

The pastoral counselor's task is to help the single adult acknowledge that a crisis is not simply an annoying mishap to be gotten rid of. A crisis can be seen as a door opener, a time to look at oneself and reevaluate oneself. Sufferers who can see a crisis as an opportunity will be able to adapt to what is happening instead of fighting it. All too often, however, people make their crises into problems to be endured, ignored, circumlocuted, anesthetized, prayed away, or cut out. The counselor can help such hurting people begin to see their crises not as demonic invaders come to cheat them or steal from them, but as unwelcome strangers with whom to make friends.

With encouragement and support, singles can learn to turn crises into steppingstones. They can learn to use the messages contained within crises to help them make the transition to their next level of unfoldment. One of my counselees expressed the principle beautifully:

> My series of crises provided me with a chance to see my dependencies. In seeing them, something happened I would not have believed possible last year when we were working through Skip's death. I somehow freed myself from him and from several other attachments that I now know were limiting my aliveness, my capacity to love anew, and my freedom as a person.
>
> Looking back at it now, I know I was kidding myself into thinking that it was primarily Skip's death that was handicapping me. It wasn't. It was *me*. It was my own inner beliefs and attitudes about myself that were trapping me. It was just like you used to say (and it made me so angry when you said it): traps are in the imagination.

Crises almost always occur when the outer supports fail and one has not yet discovered the power of the inner—one's own inner strengths, and that which theologians speak of as the Spirit of God.

One of my most precious learnings during my own single years was that often a crisis is something I unconsciously helped to create and must now consciously decipher if I am to discover a new itinerary for my journey. When I sought help from a wise counselor in the wake of my "unwanted" divorce, I was in a state of deep crisis. Once trust had been established between us, one of the first things my therapist asked was: "What are some of the things you did to drive her to divorce you?" I was furious and protested defensively. Then, as time passed, I began to see the light. If I had been sensitive over the years to the lessons contained in my marital crises, it would not have taken such a heavy confrontation to awaken me to the truth of my complicity in the demise of my marriage. In this sense a crisis might be compared to a blowout on a mountain road. At the moment, we are peeved that our journey has been spoiled or interrupted. Only later do we realize that ahead of us in the darkness was a precipice. A timely blowout can save lives.

Often the tragedy of a crisis seems to be that one has lost the fulfillment of one's cherished dreams. But that is only an apparent tragedy. The real tragedy occurs if the sufferer fails to discover who the dreamer is. In other words, the time of greatest loss is potentially also the time of greatest gain. We humans rarely reach the point of arranging for our own self-change; therefore life sometimes gives us an assist toward change. If we feel (or are) cheated, helpless, and undone, the experience can help us to remember that the disequilibrium of a crisis can be God coming to us in disguise, for God indeed comes in many garbs.

Mastering Sexuality

A ministerial colleague of mine pastors a church with the sort of storybook chapel that lovers dream about. I was not surprised when he mentioned officiating at more than 100 weddings every year in that chapel. What did capture my attention was his categorical statement that "at least 95 percent of the people I marry have previously slept together." Most of the people my friend was talking about were not libertines. The majority of them were sincere couples who came to the minister in order to be married within the context of the Christian faith. Other parish pastors have made similar estimates.* Clearly, a substantial portion of the single adults in our culture are sexually active. Even those who are not promiscuous often become sexually active when involved in a "serious" relationship, such as one in which they are considering marriage.

I am not speaking only of the young. There is a fallacious belief abroad about older people. It goes something like this: once people get older, and especially if they are single and out of practice, they lose all sexual desire. Clinically the myth is simply false; in fact nothing could be further from the truth. Research has shown that elders are anything but asexual; nor do they resemble prepubertal children, as a related myth would have it. As we view the phenomenon of older people increasingly living together, often without benefit of civil sanction or religious ceremony, we need to recognize that such relationships are often sexual as well as companionate and economically expedient.

The thought of sexual activity among nonmarried persons, whether old or young, stirs discomfort among some people. This is understandable especially when in a book about singles we come to speak of "mastering sexuality," not "mastering celibacy." Ethical issues relating to sexuality are as prominent today as ever, and it is important to face them realistically.*

One of our natural ways of being is being sexual. Sex is a natural functioning. To put it in the form of a simple theological affirmation, sex is a gift of God. One of the keystones of the Christian faith is the doctrine of creation. If it is true that God works primarily through that which God has created, then it may be stated that God can and does work through our sexual functioning. Sexual dysfunction is sometimes traceable to a person's inability or refusal to accept the fact that human sexual functioning is in essence a godly phenomenon. Even for many who have learned to say yes to this concept intellectually, there remains a deep-seated no written in their feelings and attitudes. As a pastoral counselor hardly a week goes by in which I do not touch human sexual problems. These counseling experiences suggest—and counseling colleagues and pastors corroborate—that religion is a primary cause of many sexual problems. An inflexible or otherwise inadequate set of religious-ethical beliefs leads to an unresolved feeling that sexual pleasure is sinful and to a consequent sense of self-depreciation and guilt. Sexual anxiety and dysfunction are often the result. (It goes without saying that sexual problems may also be physiologic in origin. Impotence, for instance, in a minority of cases can be caused by diabetes, alcoholism, or cardiovascular illness. For this reason a thorough physical examination should precede any counseling with respect to explicitly sexual problems.)

Healthy Sexuality

When Ron Welch first came for counseling he had no idea that he was the victim of an immature understanding of sexuality. Actually, Ron's sexuality was not his only problem, or even his main problem; it did, however, pose a major impediment to growth. Ron's story serves to focus our attention on what constitutes a healthy sexuality for single adults.

Ron came to me at his pastor's recommendation after receiving verification of what he feared most: his wife of fourteen years was involved in an affair with a married man. There was an air of desperation and urgency about Ron. He explained that he felt mortally wounded and at the end of his rope. A brilliant accountant in a managerial position, Ron was accustomed to being in control of his life. Here now was a situation in which he felt utterly out of control.

In our first session Ron wept openly for the first time in his memory. We did some crisis intervention work together—establishing rapport, giving Ron empathy and support, defining the main problem, inquiring into Ron's attempts to handle the problem, agreeing to work together, and setting minimal goals for the coming days. Because of Ron's acute distress, it seemed important to defuse the possibility of suicide. He had been giving that possibility some thought, but I learned—and these were good signs—that he had no history of suicide in his family and there had been no prior suicide gestures on his part. He agreed that he would not attempt suicide without first discussing it with me.

A few days later Ron's wife asked him to get out, stating that she intended to continue living in their house and maintaining a home for their children. When Ron suggested that she move out instead and allow him to be the custodial parent, she threatened him with a court battle, so he backed off. I was able to help him move from his home to a temporary house-sitting opportunity. We then began slowly and painfully to confront, as the weeks went by, his profound sense of "righteous indignation," as he called it. Each time Ron came for his counseling appointment he reiterated: "I feel exploited, violated, sullied." Since he had never in his life done anything morally despicable, how dare this woman whom he had trusted, the mother of his two children, do this to him? To make matters worse, facts soon came to light that during their married years Ron's wife had had several earlier affairs.

Weeks had now passed since our initial meeting. Ron's wife was definitely suing for divorce. He and I were developing a relationship of trust. One afternoon the following conversation occurred spontaneously:

Ron: I'm more than a little surprised that I feel as good as I do today. I guess I feel vindicated. You know how I've talked about not knowing what to do about Yvonne and me; after all, I am married to her and that means for life. But with all the stuff she's pulled on me, and with her filing for divorce as she has, she's taking care of it for me.

John: I don't think I understand.

Ron: She's simply proving what kind of person she really is—what she's really made of. [Pause] She told a mutual friend of ours that by God she wants what Jim can give her and she's going after it. I understand Jim's now moved out on his wife and is planning to marry Yvonne. She told this same friend that she and Jim can hardly keep their hands off of each other. [Pause] So now her true colors are coming out, for everybody to see. I think she's simply an immoral woman, has been one all along . . . you know, a sex maniac . . . nymphomaniac, isn't that the word?

John: You see Yvonne as having an unusual sex drive?

Ron: Yeah, that's for sure. I should have known better than to marry her in the first place. She told me once after we were engaged that she wasn't even a virgin. Like a fool I said that was okay, that I'd forgive and forget it. I remember that she laughed and I wondered about that at the time, but I didn't say anything. I was trying to be magnanimous. I kept thinking about Hosea, that prophet in the Old Testament, and how God told him to go ahead and marry this prostitute. [Pause] You know, all the time we were married she kept wanting more sex and more sex, crazy sex. [Pause] One time she even asked me . . . to masturbate in front of her while she watched.

John: Did you?

Ron: Are you kidding? I've never masturbated in my life.

John: Never?

Ron: Of course not. I wasn't brought up to abuse myself and dishonor God like that. [Long pause]

John: I wonder what you think you may have contributed to the gradual demise of your marriage.

Ron: [Shocked look] Like *what?*

John: I'd like you to think about that, that *what.* [Pause] Lack of warmth comes to mind as one possibility. [Long pause] Please give it some thought and let's talk about it next time.

Ron: [Very quietly] Okay.

John: I care, Ron.

Ron: I know that.

Ron was hurt by my confrontation; I could tell it as he left. I knew I had taken a risk—he might pull away from me.

Fortunately Ron didn't quit. In fact, that spontaneous con-
frontational interchange became pivotal, the first of a series
of conversations dealing with communications, feelings, intimacy, sexuality. I learned that Ron was the product of a
proper, pious Christian home, and that he had been reared
with a total lack of information about sexual matters.

As we progressed, Ron's hunger to talk about himself became rapacious. He wanted to learn, and his learnings during
the ensuing months were substantial. He read scores of books.
He enrolled in a course on human sexuality. He joined a men's
singles group with an interest in consciousness-raising. He
gradually grew to accept responsibility for his sexuality and
was able to masturbate occasionally and handle the residual
guilt associated with it. He began to see his complicity in the
failure of his marriage and to establish some close relationships with other single men and women.

Ron still needed help with three difficult tasks: dealing with
his anger over his sheltered upbringing; transforming his
childish theology into a growing spirituality; and keeping himself from prematurely remarrying. Fortunately his referring
pastor was a sensitive, supportive person. I knew Ron had
come a long way when he said, "I told my pastor that the
biggest lesson I've learned through all of this is that earthiness
is next to godliness!"

Singleness and Sexuality

In dealing with single adults one must see the broader rules
of life, not just the obvious ones. A woman whose husband
had died suddenly at the age of fifty levelled with her pastor:
"Is it really God's will that I should have no more sexual
pleasure for the rest of my life? I want to remarry but have
found no opportunity. I do not want to be promiscuous, and
I do want to be a good Christian." Her pastor might immedi-
ately have pressed for assent to a "better safe than sorry"
philosophy, or for adherence to some regulatory law. Fortunately he opted to avoid advice-giving and instead used the
occasion to learn more about the widow's life situation. Sub-

sequently he referred her to a woman counselor, recognizing that a male pastor may not be in the best position to counsel a single woman with respect to decisions about the expressing of her sexuality.

We do not know how Jesus dealt with his sexuality personally. We do know that he was fully human. We also know that his message included the proclamation of love as God's law for all people and of grace as the primary characteristic of God's relationship to humankind. In this light it seems doubtful that Jesus meant for Christians to deny their sexuality. On the contrary, in the Fourth Gospel he is quoted as saying: "I have come that they may have life, and may have it in all its fullness" (John 10:10b NEB).

James B. Nelson has extensively considered the matter of sexual expression for Christians.* He sets forth three general principles that he regards as appropriate norms for decision:

> First, love requires a single standard and not a double standard for sexual morality. . . . Love must always be expressed as justice. Without justice it becomes individualistic and shallowly sentimental. . . . Love expressed as justice becomes the lively concern for the empowerment of all persons, so that everyone has rightful access to the means for human fulfillment. This implies that there cannot be one sexual ethic for males and another for females, nor one for the unmarried and another for the married. . . . The same basic considerations of love ought to apply to all.
>
> Second, the physical expression of one's sexuality with another person ought to be appropriate to the level of loving commitment present in that relationship. Our relationships exist on a continuum—from the fleeting and casual to the lasting and intense, from the relatively impersonal to the deeply personal. So also physical expressions exist on a continuum—from varied types of eye contact and casual touch, to varied forms of embrace and kiss, to bodily caresses, to petting and foreplay, to the different forms of sexual intercourse. In some way or another we inevitably express our sexuality in every human relationship. The morality of that expression . . . will depend upon its appropriateness to the shared level of commitment and the nature of the relationship itself.
>
> Third, genital sexual expression should be evaluated in regard to motivations, intentions, the nature of the act itself,

and the consequences of the act, each of these informed and shaped by love.*

Following an elaboration of the several aspects of this third principle, Nelson adds:

> Some readers will want to lay claim to more specific sexual rules in addition to guiding principles such as these. If so, well and good. I personally find certain sexual rules important and useful. I do not view them as exceptionless absolutes, but I presume strongly in their favor, and the burden of proof is then on me to justify any exception by its greater faithfulness to the higher loyalty. Rules can protect us at the boundaries of our experience where we encounter our limitations in knowledge and wholeness. But however sexual rules are used, they should nurture our growth into greater maturity and responsible freedom, and not inhibit it.
>
> To love is to be open to life. Nowhere is this more evident than in the directly sexual forms of our loving.†

Jesus spoke of what he called the kingdom of God—a future wholeness, a society of shalom within the human family circle. As Christians we are called to cocreate the kingdom. If the kingdom of God is to be characterized by spiritual, emotional, mental, social, and environmental wholeness, it is certain also to be characterized by sexual wholeness within the family of humankind. More than the other kinds of wholeness, sexual wholeness is threatening to many. This is not surprising when one remembers how threatening other movements toward wholeness have been—equal rights for women, for example. Most ministers, aware that sexuality is an important subject for singles, are willing to deal with it despite its being threatening to unsingles as well as singles. However, before attempting to care for single adults in their sexual needfulness, it is wise for the minister to: (1) become knowledgeable about human sexuality in general; (2) be familiar with some useful models for helping people make difficult ethical and moral decisions; and (3) deal with one's own sexuality so that the sexual and intimacy needs of the counselor do not impinge upon those of counselees.

Many singles do not remain single forever, and that is all right. However, singles who have made peace with their sexuality are less likely to rush into mating (including marriage) relationships just to satisfy frustrated sexual appetites.

Mastering Unsingleness

There has been a steady increase in ministerial divorces over the past decade, and divorced clergy—I am referring here to male clergy—tend to remarry speedily, on the average within one year.* Only rarely does a divorced minister take the time needed to complete the grief process that normally follows so significant a loss. Many of these single clergymen who remarry quickly do so for debatable reasons—out of lonesomeness, to have help with housekeeping and entertaining, because pastoral placement is difficult for unmarried ministers, or because they need an alter ego or a church organist. Of course, some divorced clergy also choose singlehood, and others remarry for healthier reasons than those just given. I have known ministers who have truly grieved efficiently and even done a remarkable amount of anticipatory grief work prior to their divorce. Many have come to see and admit that they were irresponsible to their previous spouse—perhaps out of a desire to complete their education or build their professional reputation—and they are not making the same mistake in their new marriage. These ministers may indeed have been ready for remarriage in less than a year. Sadly, I also know of a number of second divorces among ministers who apparently remarried before they were adequately prepared. I believe that preparation for marriage ought to include a substantial period of singlehood. The best time to master unsingleness is during singlehood.

The most common form of unsingleness, of course, is formal marriage. Sooner or later most people marry at least once. Most of them marry wisely and well. But many marry prematurely. This is reflected in the mounting number of unsatisfying marriages and unwanted divorces. Perhaps a consideration of unsingleness and the need for mastering it outside the so-called bonds of matrimony can shed light on why some marriages fail.

To master the art of unsingleness requires that we become

skilled at relating in mutuality and love—love of self as well as others—and to gain proficiency in human communication generally. This can be more readily accomplished by non-married people than by married people because the skills involved are easiest to acquire through the experiential, inductive learning processes that come from a *variety* of relationships. Such experiential learning requires the kind of time and energy and experimentation that may be more available to singles than to married people.

The notion of singles mastering unsingleness resulted from my friendship with a woman in the Midwestern United States. We met at a singles conference where, as one of the speakers and resource persons, I did some brief counseling with her in the wake of her divorce. She asked for my address and wrote me occasionally, sharing her journey with me. Her letters evidenced steady growth over the next couple of years, and I wrote to tell her so. In a letter written about three years after our only face-to-face meeting, she summarized her learnings:

> I have learned a great deal about "marriage" during this "unmarried" time. I want to learn even more about it, all I can know. I want to know what marriage *is* for today's world, and *why* it is what it is, and *how to tell* when it might work and when it might not. And I want to know (I know living is taking risks) what to do about it—shy of another formal ceremony destined to end in another divorce. I know my failure in marriage left me traumatized and gun-shy, but that has been a blessing. I'm still single (hooray) and I've learned so much. Anyway, with the help of therapy and caring friends, I think most of the fears are behind me now.
>
> The past couple years I feel like I've had a series of increasingly successful relationships, like mini-marriages; and I truly am open now to the possibility of a permanent relationship. But I don't *have* to have one. I want to be well-married to me, first. Then I want to keep learning how to be well-married to others (the women and men who've become so precious to me), second. And then maybe, just maybe, I will be free to (and will want to) choose to get well-married to one special person . . . third.

Creative Singlehood

My friend was learning, as a single, how to be unsingle. The following thoughts about the kinship between singlehood and unsingleness are intended as guidelines for all singles, though their pertinence may be greater for persons who are single by death or divorce, those singles who, generalizing from their own experience, tend to equate unsingleness with marriage. The counseling process has its "teachable moments." In such moments you may wish to share these ideas either for immediate discussion or for the counselee to ponder.

Self-Love

First, creative singlehood and creative unsingleness are interdependent. Usually people who are good at one are also good at the other. As we have seen, the prime requisite for being well-married to another person is being *well-married to oneself*. This concept is basic to creative singlehood. It is also basic to creative unsingleness. The key word, of course, is "self." One who is well-married to self is self-preserving, self-supporting, self-fulfilling, self-loving.

Self-love stands in sharp contrast to all narcissism. Narcissism, alarmingly prevalent in contemporary society, is a pseudo-self-love that actually keeps people from becoming well-married to themselves. While all of us may be narcissistic at times or to some degree, real narcissists are unable to love. They cannot love themselves and thus are incapable of loving others. They find it difficult, perhaps impossible, to relate in nonexploitive ways and to make long-term commitments.

I learned about narcissism the hard way. I once knew and tried to love a vibrant, charming narcissist whose demands (that I defer my needs and give attention only to those of the narcissist) were so subtle that for a long time I failed to discern the inequity. Finally I learned, painfully, that true lovers of self prize equally their own freedom and worthfulness and that of others. Narcissists live as if they value chiefly such things as immediate gratification and avoidance of pain. Only healthy self-love can foster a singlehood creative enough to move toward love of others and, ultimately, love of God as in Jesus' Great Commandment: "You must love the Lord your God with your whole heart, your whole soul, your whole strength, and your whole mind, and your neighbor as your-self" (Luke 10:27, Goodspeed translation).

Choice

Second, the more one masters unsingleness, the freer one is to remain single by choice. Some of the healthiest people I know, people who are well-married to themselves, speak of freely choosing singlehood. Among them are a friend who is a Roman Catholic priest and a woman who has been a widow for thirty-five years. I think of them as living examples of human wellness. Fulfilled persons at peace with their single-hood, they are at the same time highly skilled at unsingle-ness; that is, they have a number of relationships character-ized by mutual closeness. In a sense, then, a new type of singlehood has emerged as a positive life style in our times, that well-married-to-self singlehood which is freely chosen. This kind of singlehood is an increasingly acceptable option in today's society.

There are reasons why such a singlehood is more possible and desirable now than ever before. Three are worth mention-ing here: (1) the urbanization, overpopulation, and increased longevity which make marriage and procreation less crucial for personal survival and the survival of humankind; (2) adult education and career change or development which are now regarded as possible and even normative for persons in midlife or beyond and often easier for nonmarried persons; and (3) the phenomenon of women choosing permanent sin-glehood as the most healthful way for them to live in a pre-dominantly sexist society.*

Autonomy

Third, marriage in the traditional sense certainly remains an option for today. However, it is becoming more and more difficult to build and sustain such a marriage. Couples are bearing fewer children to bind them together; people are liv-ing longer than ever; and women are no longer as dependent on husbands to meet their identity needs and security needs.

Today the good marriages I know are "good" because each spouse is well-married to herself or himself. They hold their partnership as a couple in dynamic tension with their respective autonomy as individuals. Of course, it is appropriate for spouses to emphasize their unsingleness skills, even as non-married persons tend to emphasize their singlehood skills. But both sets of skills are present in each of us since everyone carries within an inevitable tension between the thrust toward autonomy and the pull toward relatedness.

Essential Skills

It appears, then, that the skills needed for creative singlehood and those needed for creative unsingleness are essentially the same. At least they overlap to a large degree. It is simplest to illustrate this principle within the context of marriage, the most familiar form of unsingleness.

In the first place, persons who combine healthy singlehood with a healthy marriage seem to bring to one another the ability to solve problems as they arise, the ability to handle feelings (especially hostile feelings), the ability to negotiate issues related to power and control, and the ability to define and redefine roles as needed. In short they are skilled at non-defensive negotiating, even in a live-in partnership where so much is at stake.

Next, the best marriages I know are no longer haunted by the ghosts of yesteryear. The partners do not dump hurtful, blameful garbage on their mates—refuse that belongs, if it belongs anywhere, on ex-spouses, mothers, fathers, employers. On the contrary, these are people who at least in part are well-married to each other because they long ago divorced their respective parents and former spouses emotionally. They do not need to fight their way out of their childhood homes or other former relationships. They do not need to use their mate as the nearest object on which to project their unfinished business with the past. Some of these good marriages, incidentally, are second or third marriages. But whether the earlier relationships ended by death, desertion, or divorce, the present partners have made peace with past relationships. A rule of thumb suggests itself for singles contemplating a new mating relationship: whoever cannot tolerate the presence of an ex-lover or ex-spouse—whether by letter, photo, telephone, or face-to-face—has not yet emotionally separated from that person.

Finally, good marriages seem to have in common one other main ingredient, namely "mutualities." One of the married couples I know exemplifies this well. They have similar personal values, compatible work values, comparable intellectual gifts, and a common religious commitment. They are both intense persons, sexually attracted to each other, and respectful of each other's talents and skills. The result is an essentially enjoyable relationship instead of an enervating uphill climb. They are witness to the fact that only with a high degree of mutuality can two (or more) people sustain a high degree of mutual need satisfaction.

One of the finest masters of unsingleness I ever met has written: "Without mutual willingness of me as a self to affirm you as a self, no meeting is possible—no encounter, no loving. And until there is mutuality in our attempts to encounter one another, I alone (or you alone) can do nothing to make 'meeting' happen. In other words, loving/meeting happens within the context of mutuality or not at all."* To put it another way: to master unsingleness is to master mutuality, the art of loving encounter.

To be creatively single, then, ultimately involves the same survival skills and mastery skills as are necessary for creative *un*singleness. It is wise to acquire them in singlehood. It is also hard to do. However, the acquisition of these skills is even more difficult for the person who has entered into a marriage contract without being well-married to self—that is, without first mastering both singlehood and unsinglehood.

4. Launching a Singles Ministry

Two single adults were having lunch together. Part of their conversation focused on the church:

"I'd love to have you come to church with me this Sunday."

"I'd like to, but as far as God is concerned I'm definitely beyond redemption."

"What do you mean?"

"You know what I mean."

"No, I really don't know what you mean."

"Are you kidding? You know the way I've played around."

"God knows how to play."

"Not the God at my church."

"Look, I'm not asking you to go to your church; I'm asking you to come with me to mine."

[Pause] "Do you have any idea how long it's been since I darkened the door of a church? God himself would faint!"

"Look, we've got a dancing God who's never fainted yet. [Pause] Please come with me. You'll like the people in the singles group, and our pastor is a tremendous person."

"Okay, okay! I'll try it once, but only because you're my friend . . . and so persistent. But I still think I'm beyond redemption."

As this lively dialogue implies, some singles make wonderful lay evangelists. Once sold on their ministry, they will speak out fearlessly. In fact, if just a handful of singles with leadership gifts becomes convinced that your church really cares about them and isn't judging them or putting them down, that you as their pastor are committed to investing yourself in their lives and that a church-related singles' support system is a good idea, nothing will stop them from promoting their ministry wherever they are—at work, on the telephone with friends, or at a social gathering.

However, there are some hurdles to surmount in order to launch a singles ministry. Developing a self-supporting ministry to single adults requires lots of energy and much patience. And once a pastor succeeds in establishing such a ministry there is even more work to be done, such as counseling and caring for its constituency. Therefore busy pastors will want first to ask in all honesty: "Do I really want to do this? How much emphasis do I want to place on reaching out to single adults? With all the other worthwhile priorities in my pastorate, why add yet another?" A half-hearted commitment will be known at once—and judged accordingly.

The Challenge

An NBC White Paper on the status of the American family reported that in a single year recently one million people in the United States became divorced, one-fifth of all families were now single-parent families, and "within the past decade there has been an increase of 6 million people who have decided to live alone."* On the same telecast it was also stated that there are now more single-parent homes in America than there are "traditional" families, those in which the father is the breadwinner and the mother stays home to care for the children.

The change in family patterning has important implications. According to one source, "We are living in a family-oriented society in which couples are the norm. Singles are often stereotyped, misunderstood, or treated as outsiders. This is unfair. It discriminates against an important minority, 40 percent of the U.S. adult population, nearly 50 million people."† The same source indicates that about half of these 50 million singles have never married. The other half are separated, divorced, or single by death. Many singles are raising families under difficult circumstances, especially the 60 percent of single adults who are women.

Obviously, then, the need for a ministry of pastoral care and counseling among single adults is great at this time. Indications are that the need will continue to grow.

Still, not every pastor will want to place special emphasis on a ministry to singles, nor does one "have to." There is plenty of important ministerial work to be done without tackling this particular kind of apostolate. If you are a pastor, perhaps the present discussion can help you decide whether a special outreach to singles makes sense for you and your congregation at this time.

Making Contact

Before making contact with single adults, several prerequisites need be in place—in combination: (1) a pastor who particularly cares about singles and wants to minister to them; (2) a congregation of people willing to extend themselves, personally and financially, in order to reach out to nonmarried adults; and (3) a nucleus of singles who are already related to the church and want to share their lives and faith with other singles. Too often, singles in the church have either been peripheral to the life of the congregation, or cliquish and reticent to reach out to unchurched singles. Too often, also, pastors and congregations have been too insensitive to care or too fearful to act.

The best time to make initial contact with singles may well be when they are newly single. This is when they are most accessible. The emotional condition of the newly single person is often one of disorientation. Other feelings may include distress, shame, guilt, embarrassment, hypersensitivity, disappointment, moodiness, worry over financial matters, and lonesomeness. On the other hand, the newly single person may feel relief, elation, even "born again" in the sense of having a new lease on life. Newly single adults are often hungry for new friendships, and adventure, or help from someone who accepts them and cares.

Even singles who have always been single or who over the years have recovered from postdeath or postdivorce crises may be leading lives of frustration or quiet despair. They may be wishing for some activity to refresh their spirits. They too will respond to caring overtures.

In both individual and group counseling settings, singles have reported that they frequently think about God, religion, and the church. When they do, their thoughts and feelings are mixed. Beliefs they learned in childhood often resurface in conscious awareness, especially in the wake of divorce; more often than not these beliefs are inadequate or negative. On the other hand, there is a longing for something worth believing, a God who cares, a giving and accepting community. Some singles are grasping for help with personal survival. Others want a way to revive their fractured faith in God and the goodness of life. Still others want to learn self-support skills. If lovingly contacted, many singles will give the church a fair chance to minister to them. If they find useful programming and a support network of new friends, some of them will become part of the church's ministry to other singles.

Guidelines

In order for the church to care effectively for singles once it has established contact with them, it must have something to offer that the singles want. In the main, the church must offer programming that meets their needs, and a community that can nurture healing and growth. Participation in the church must be of practical usefulness to singles. It must help them move toward a greater degree of wellness as persons, or they will drop out.

The guidelines sketched here are based on my observation of church-related singles groups that seem to be ministering effectively. They are offered to pastors, congregations, and singles who want to minister to single adults.

First, the most productive singles ministries are offered not by well-meaning pastors or congregations but by single women and men themselves. They are ministries of, as well as by and for, the single laity. Such ministries occur in groups of single adults who know each other, care for each other, love one another, challenge one another, and band together to invest unbelievable amounts of time and energy in their vocation as paraprofessional ministers to other singles in their communities. Typically they enjoy ongoing pastoral mentorship and support, or at least good will, from the congregations to which they are related, but they—the singles themselves—are indeed the ministers.

Second, such singles ministries are rarely initiated by these same laity, though it would obviously be of help to the initiating pastor to invite some singles to collaborate in planning and implementing such a program from the outset. Normally the impetus begins with the church staff or congregation who, seeing a need in their community, place that vision high among their priorities and see to it that it receives pastoral attention, staff time, careful planning, and adequate funding. Once the singles ministry takes root, the professional church leaders wisely step into the background, encouraging the singles themselves to organize, elect officers and boards or committees, formulate a budget, and function autonomously under church sponsorship.

Third, effective singles ministries are clearly identified with, and closely related to, a particular local congregation. A singles ministry seems to thrive better with a home base and a sense of belonging—rooted in an extended family with a name and a heritage. Some of the most exciting groups I have seen are "wildly ecumenical" within their own membership, embracing singles from many religious traditions as well as from none at all; but they always seem self-consciously to identify themselves as "The First Presbyterian Church Singles" (or Baptist, or Methodist, or Community Church). Singles groups often attend worship services together. They encourage individual members to join the choir, teach in the church school, and participate in interchurch athletic leagues. In other words, the local church provides more than a gathering place; it serves as an operational base that offers ongoing programs to attend and opportunities for discovering and using personal talents. With this congregational foundation in place special programs for singles can be developed to supplement what the church already offers.

Fourth, many successful singles ministries incorporate an explicitly educational thrust. Some groups have at their core a weekly church school class; that is especially true in the so-called evangelical churches. At First Baptist Church in Topeka, Kansas, the "SASS Class" is the largest class in the entire educational program and a mainstay of a highly visible singles outreach that incorporates a number of different approaches. ("SASS" is an acronym for "Single Adult Sunday School.") For singles unable to attend on Sunday because of schedule conflicts, a duplicate class session is held on a weekday evening. Such classes often focus on biblical studies geared to single adult issues. In some churches a popular format has involved the use of guest teachers from the community—perhaps college professors or mental health professionals—in a series of presentations. A short course on "Making Difficult Ethical Decisions as a Single" is likely to evoke interest. Some singles ministries not centered in a church school class may be education-oriented nonetheless, offering conferences, workshops, retreats, short-term seminars, and formal or informal courses of instruction. To capitalize on the current popularity of adult education, some groups affiliate with a nearby college as an extension center and are thereby enabled to offer accredited courses. One singles group has sponsored courses in "Human Sexuality," "Living the Single Life Creatively," "Psychology of Religion," and "How to Love and Be Loved." Some groups have offered such educational activities as folk-dancing classes, meditation and relaxation workshops, assertiveness training, and yoga—all under church auspices.

Fifth, effective singles ministries actively recruit new members. Such recruiting may be necessary for survival inasmuch as many singles move to other cities or become unsingle and drop out. But for whatever reason, successful singles groups are characteristically zealous, whether from the standpoint of "evangelical salvation" or "social salvation" or both. They strongly believe in what they are offering and they eagerly share their "good news" with anyone who will listen. They also seem willing to follow through faithfully on contacting prospects. Social events opened to the community at large often involve a recruitment concern. A dinner dance, a nature hike, a ski weekend—all can help promote the singles organization. Some singles groups include evangelism-training workshops among their regular program offerings.

Sixth, vital singles groups are characteristically well organized. Their leaders include a cadre of persons who bring to their lay ministry a variety of backgrounds, as well as a lively circle of contacts outside the church. One group's steering committee had two educators, a physician, an architect, and a prominent retailer among its women members; the men on the committee were also talented and capable people. When I was invited to speak at a weekend retreat sponsored by this particular group, I was impressed with their commitment to ministry, their relaxed efficiency, and their high energy level. While one of the pastors of their church attended and gave spiritual guidance to the group, it was obvious that these laymen and laywomen assumed full responsibility for their ministry to each other as singles.

Seventh, church-related singles groups that are effective are marked by a pervasive emphasis on spirituality. Theirs is a tolerant, open spirituality set within the context of single living and expressed in biblical and theological study groups, prayer groups, and growth groups. They often enjoy group singing of classic religious songs, but also of secular songs that convey a spiritual message ("I've Got to Be Me," "Bridge Over Troubled Water," "The Impossible Dream"). Along with the emphasis on spiritual growth, however, there is a definite psychological emphasis. Indeed this psychological dimension is closely integrated with the spiritual dimension. In some groups the singles speak psychologically as easily or more easily than they do theologically. They readily speak of being in therapy or having been in therapy, and they seem to favor therapists who are either connected with their group or informally endorsed by it.

This dual emphasis on the psychological and the theological usually reflects their mentoring pastor's high interest in both areas. In most thriving church-related singles organizations, spiritual growth and psychotherapy are seen as congruent and even mutually interdependent. This does not seem a forced posture or one that has been explicitly promoted, but rather a natural byproduct of the life and values of the group.

Eighth, singles ministries that last over the years foster a broad outreach. They plan for a variety of special interest groups and activities. Flourishing groups often have a sizable contingent of elders, single parents, recovering alcoholics, and never married singles. They go out of their way to be sure that no one feels unwelcome. I heard of several singles who spent their Saturday at church constructing a ramp adjacent to the stairway that leads to their meeting room, even though no paraplegics or other handicapped singles yet belonged to their group; soon after, however, their meetings included a few persons in wheelchairs. I have seen singles sponsor a chapter of Alcoholics Anonymous, a gourmet club, a task force on world hunger, a backpacking club, a "Single Singers" chorale, and a handbell choir. The possibilities are endless.

Ninth and finally, effective church-related singles groups see to it that the "tone" of their organization remains one of non-exploitive caring. One of the chief purposes for the creation of a singles ministry is that it can provide a valuable alternative to singles' bars and singles' organizations where the tone is quite different. Single women, especially, often complain that some singles groups are de facto "meat markets" where most if not all of the men are there mainly to "score." This is exasperating and offensive to sensitive singles—both men and women—in search of friendship and growth in a nonthreatening atmosphere, one in which they will not be pushed to prostitute themselves. If a singles ministry establishes and maintains such a caring atmosphere, it will succeed. If it does not, it will fail. Single adults who are saddened by the lack of humane organizations that speak to their needs ought to consider starting one of their own within the context of their church. If their own church is not interested, they can find a church that is!

I have highlighted nine key features of the singles ministries I have observed. No one group embodies all of them. However, any church-related singles program can try to incorporate a majority of them in an effort to fulfill its ministry.

The Minister as Counselor to Singles

Ministers who would pastor single adults need to prepare themselves for the task. Special skills and understandings need to be acquired, especially by clergypersons who hope to be pastoral *counselors* to singles.

Awareness

Pastoral counselors, but especially clergy*men,* need to understand women in general and single women in particular. In fact any male pastor who would counsel single women ought first to be well oriented in feminist thought and concerns and in the psychology of women. At least he ought to become aware of how, when, and to whom to refer single women needing the kinds of help he cannot give himself. Because of the double standard and sexism of our culture, for example, single women often experience a greater diminishing of their self-esteem than do their male counterparts. It is implied, or they may be flatly told, that in their singlehood they are double or triple failures: they have failed to prove themselves sexually attractive; they have been inadequate wives and homemakers, the traditional badges of femininity; and they have probably not succeeded in their professional careers either—at least not in comparison with men of the same age. In this way single women in our society are subjected to a far more judgmental "put-down" than single men.

The point is that the experiences of single women and single men in our society show some characteristic differences. Pastors need to be aware of these differences, even though in this book I have focused more on the similarities than the dis-

similarities among singles. This focus is not without justifica-
tion. There is more androgyny in today's culture than ever
before, and in many instances single adults are living on the
frontiers of androgynous experience. A simple example is the
fact that some single women now feel free to ask a man for a
date, or to send him flowers. However, some differences do
exist, and frequently have to be reckoned with. The pastoral
counselor ought to be aware of and sensitive to the different
ways men and women view and experience their singlehood.

Singles, especially when they feel hurt, angry, or insecure,
sometimes adopt certain pervasive but fallacious notions that
need to be challenged: men are independent, women dependent; men are sexual, women spiritual; men are stronger than
women; men are logical, whereas women are emotional; men
are forthright and trustworthy, while women are apt to gossip
or lie (about their age, for example); men are smarter than
women (aren't the world's greatest scientists, scholars, and
chefs men?). Indeed such myths ought clearly to be disavowed.
The truth may well be the exact opposite of what these "big
lies" assert. My counseling experience at any rate suggests that
in some substantial ways single women are clearly more independent, more rational, more honest, and stronger than single
men.

My new awareness began when I was interviewing a con-
siderable number of separated spouses who were under the
care of pastoral counselors. This research disclosed not only
similarities but also some striking differences between the husbands and wives: the female respondents tended toward elation
in their separation, while the males tended towards depression;
the women found it easier to lean on others than did the men;
there was a strong tendency for separated men to make changes
in their sexual behavior (more masturbation, for instance),
whereas the separated women reported no change; males increased significantly the time and energy they expended on
household and personal maintenance tasks, while females took
on few, if any, new tasks; and separated husbands admitted to

a higher degree of general anxiety than did separated wives. In addition, males reported diminished physical well-being and deterioration in such ingestive habits as eating, smoking, and drinking; females did not.* Women consistently emerged in that study as anything but "the weaker sex."

Openness

Ministers are in a unique position when it comes to helping singles. That position has both advantages and disadvantages. Much depends on the pastor's openness to singles ministry.

On the positive side, single-by-death persons usually come into contact with a minister soon after their spouse dies, whether they are leaning on their own pastor or using a minister suggested by the funeral director. During the period when their marriage is ending, separated spouses or single-by-divorce persons often turn to the minister who performed their wedding ceremony. In these ways ministers are given early opportunity to make contact with singles. Pastors who are competent to counsel such persons effectively and channel them into a church-related singles group can often meet real needs and enlarge the scope of their ministry.

However, capitalizing on an initial contact with singles in crisis can often be difficult. It requires a great deal of understanding and relational skills on the part of the minister and a great deal of openness. Sometimes nothing works. In fact, singles sometimes do all they can to avoid the pastor who married them because they feel too guilty to face the person who made marriage sound so idyllic, so glorious, and so irrevocable. Some singles are simply embarrassed. Others may actually fear pastoral punishment!

I once counseled Susan, a divorced woman whose pastor had advised against her marrying Gerald. Once Pastor Forrest realized how determined she was to marry the man despite anybody's objections, he went ahead and performed the marriage anyway. It was evidently a beautiful wedding ceremony, done with a "flourish" and a built-in "preachment" (her terms) admonishing the young couple to take their vows seriously. After the marriage failed, Susan was positive that her pastor would scold and say, "I told you so," so she dropped out of the church completely. Once our counseling reached the point where I could be sure of Susan's trust, I told her that I knew Pastor Forrest well and believed him to be sensitive and forgiving. Eventually she and her pastor reconciled.

Ministers face yet another disadvantage as counselors: once a decision is made by either spouse, or both, to end the marriage, couples tend to give up on marriage counseling. All marriage counselors face this problem, but ministers may be especially vulnerable because they are viewed as people who promote marriage, perform weddings, baptize or consecrate children, and frown on divorce. The transition from marriage counseling to divorce counseling can be a tricky one for counselor and counselee alike. In fact it may be impossible if the counselor has implied all along that every marriage ought to be saved at all costs, or if the minister has portrayed an idealized and unrealistic picture of marriage. I once heard a well-known pastor say to a group of young married couples: "Anybody can make a marriage succeed if they work at it hard enough." What he said is simply untrue! Ministers need to ask themselves early on and at a fundamental level whether they want people to look to them for care and counseling at all times and in all situations, or only when things are going well.

There is no unique or special approach to counseling single adults. Any method that establishes and deepens relationships and then facilitates personal growth in a context of openness, caring, and loving confrontation can be effective. However, there are some pitfalls and stumbling blocks that pastoral counselors of single adults would be well advised to avoid.

Pitfalls

First, avoid planting a "mine field" that you may need to traverse yourself at a later time. The "mines" to which I refer are statements made from the pulpit, or in personal dialogue and premarital interviews, or in mailings and parish papers, or even in casual conversation at social gatherings. In such statements it is easy to imply inadvertently that marriage is God's will for all normal people, that divorce is an awful shame, and that you feel sorry for those whom one minister actually refers to as "unclaimed blessings"—those "poor souls" who have never found a spouse. It is wise to think through carefully and know clearly what you really believe about marriage, divorce, and singlehood. Then, be precise in what you say: say what you mean and mean what you say. If you are married, being candid about the joys and struggles in your own marriage can serve to humanize you in the eyes of your parishioners. People already know that life is difficult, and being truthful about its difficulties is good pastoral practice. The point is that it is easier to help counselees move from marriage counseling to divorce counseling, or postdivorce grief counseling, if you have not previously created a fairy-tale picture of love and marriage that acts as a barrier between you and parishioners in need.

Second, avoid letting your best assets stunt your counselees' growth. Ministers attracted to pastoral counseling are typically caring, sensitive, idealistic, intuitive, sympathetic persons who are warmed by approval and often let the heart overrule the head. These characteristics can all be pastoral strengths, but they can also be liabilities. Many male ministers have learned the hard way about the dangers of sexual transference by needy female counselees going through separation and divorce, and about their personal vulnerability as they are truly concerned for the needs of such counselees. The dangers are especially acute if the pastor's own sexual needs and needs for closeness and intimacy are not being adequately met in his marriage or friendships. Women are drawn to sensitive men, and sensitive men are drawn to the role of rescuer. As more and more women become pastoral practitioners, they too will have to beware of a similar peril in their counseling of men. Cocounseling by male and female pastors, and reciprocal referral between them, are increasingly available options.

Male counselors again need to be aware of a third danger. Single women entering counseling or therapy often need specifically to learn to trust their own feelings and perceptions. They need to get in touch with their own power and take responsibility for their own decisions. Some women are tempted instead to give their power away to a warm, understanding, "wise" male therapist. Male pastors dare not let their women counselees do this. If you have difficulty keeping them from it, or keeping yourself from telling them what they ought to do, refer them promptly, preferably to a female counselor. As we have already noted, a male minister is often not the best person to do long-term counseling with women, especially single women. Sometimes he must, for he may be the best or even the only available resource person. But women need to identify with women counselors who are role models of warmth, spirituality, and strength. Women pastors and therapists can understand the experience of women in our culture from the inside, in ways that even aware and sensitive men cannot. When skilled women counselors can be found, they ought to be used.

Fourth, avoid trying to do all the counseling yourself, or to do your particular counseling all by yourself. Peer counseling is especially helpful for singles. For example, a woman who has recovered from her husband's death can offer excellent care for new widows. Growth and support groups for single-by-choice persons render real service. So do postdivorce grief groups. Divorcing persons can even be invited to participate in an ongoing grief group for widows and widowers! As to your personal counseling practice, by all means seek out a consultant who can provide ongoing supervision, or join a "therapy group for therapists" in order to meet your own needs for professional growth and personal pastoral care. If you cannot find an appropriate group to join, start one. Too many ministers operate as "soloists," concealing or denying their own needs for care. The need for care is a normal part of all creation, and that need is inexorable. We ministers are no exception, and counseling pastors are in particular need of ongoing care.

Enrichment

Pastoral counselors will find a cluster of understandings and techniques within the larger counseling field that can enrich their work with single adults. You might wish to focus your personal reading and/or continuing education plans in order to strengthen your skills in one or more of the following areas of special interest and concern:

Crisis Intervention Theory and Methodology
Career Assessment (Vocational Guidance)
Human Sexuality and Sex Therapy
Psychology of Women
Psychology of Men
Assertiveness Training
Group Dynamics and Group Counseling
Single Parenting and Family Therapy
Suicidology
Treatment of Depression
Stress Management
Time Management
Financial Planning
Thanatology (Death, Dying, and Grief)

Obviously no one can hope to master all of these areas of expertise, especially if one must simultaneously maintain the generalist's portfolio required in the parish pastorate. An up-to-date file of ready referral resources is essential. Single adults themselves are usually happy to tell their pastor who or what has been helpful to them.

A final suggestion for pastors who want to minister effectively to singles: that ministry can be enriched if you foster a congregational attitude that is positively disposed toward single adults. I have seen pastors abandon their ministry to singles in face of the flak coming at them from important church members. Single laypersons have become discouraged in their efforts to reach out to other singles when they felt unsupported

by their own church family. Such troubles can be prevented
through careful attention to the relationship between the needs
of singles and those of the larger congregation.

Two young women nearing their thirties were overheard
chatting at an after-worship coffee hour:

> Clara: If living together with Keith when I love him so much
> is sinful, how about living with someone you've never
> ever loved at all? That's what I wonder about.
>
> Carolyn: I suppose a lot of people do that for security or
> money or any number of reasons.
>
> Clara: Well, it's what my own mother says she has done for
> thirty-five years. Does her having said "I do" in front of
> some justice of the peace, because she was pregnant and
> thought she'd better get married, make her righteous?
> Keith and I have said "I do" to each other and before
> God, but not in front of a minister or justice of the peace.
> Does that make us automatically *un*righteous?
>
> Carolyn: I don't know, but I would really like to know more
> about you and Keith, and how you got together.
>
> Clara: Wow, that's funny. I thought you'd judge me.
>
> Carolyn: I don't feel any need to judge you. I got married
> ten years ago right in front of this church sanctuary, and
> I didn't have nearly as good a reason as you seem to have
> for living with Keith. I just felt I had to get away from
> my parents. Luckily it seems to be working out; George
> and I seem to love each other more now than we did then.
>
> Clara: I'm glad.
>
> Carolyn: I'm glad you've started to come to our church. I
> hope you'll keep coming, and Keith too.

Carolyn accepted Clara, and it is easy to imagine their becoming friends.

Singles will feel welcome if your parishioners welcome
them, and they will feel at home in your church if they find
themselves among people with a breadth of perspective and

depth of soul. Such a church will be able to integrate single adults fully into their common life on the basis of equality. Church people can learn to minister effectively to each other as members of an extended family. When they do, the distinction between persons who are single and those who are not will fade into insignificance.

A main thesis of this book has been that creative pastoral care and counseling are important for creative singlehood. If singles are to sort out their experience in an integrative way and move toward wholeness and a high level of well-being, they need help. With good help, they can achieve good growth —emotionally, interpersonally, spiritually, and in other important ways—with less of the lonesome and vacuous existence many singles presently suffer, and with less of a need to run away from singlehood. With godly help singles may even come to find God in their singlehood.

Notes

Page

3. *There are exceptions. For example, losing one's mate through suicide usually results in embarrassment and a state of crisis. In such a case, the dynamics of singlehood may be more like those of divorced persons.

3. †I have borrowed the term "good grief" from Granger E. Westberg, whose book *Good Grief* has helped many grieving persons.

4. *There are exceptions. For example, if a person's dying is a long and protracted process and the surviving spouse does anticipatory grief work, the mourner may at the moment of death already be far along the road to recovery. Also, single-by-death people often marry friends they have known for years, thus mitigating the need for an extended courtship.

6. *I am indebted to Howard W. Stone for his articulation of these dynamics in *Suicide and Grief* (Philadelphia: Fortress Press, 1972). See also Wayne E. Oates, *Pastoral Care and Counseling in Grief and Separation* for a more exhaustive treatment of grief phenomena, including anticipatory grief.

7. *Webster's Third New International Dictionary of the English Language Unabridged*, 1961.

8. *A concise elaboration of this idea and its implications is found in chapter 13 of Howard J. Clinebell, *Basic Types of Pastoral Counseling* (Nashville: Abingdon, 1966). For an in-depth treatment see Edward V. Stein, *Guilt: Theory and Therapy* (Philadelphia: Westminster Press, 1968).

11. *In *Anger and Assertiveness in Pastoral Care* David W. Augsburger deals with this topic in a useful and comprehensive manner. His volume is directed especially to clergy, many of whom tend to avoid their own anger.

15. *Ibid.

16. *For a simple but thorough primer on the topic, see Stone, *Crisis Counseling*.

19. *Random House Dictionary of the English Language*, unabridged edition, 1966.

21. *U.S. statistics reported in the *San Francisco Chronicle*, January 30, 1980.

25. *Random House Dictionary.*
27. *M. Scott Peck, *The Road Less Traveled* (New York: Simon and Schuster, 1978), p. 168.
27. †I do not believe that people fall in and out of love; rather they choose to grow in love with one another, or they choose not to. I use the term "in love" here because of the head-over-heels feelings implied.
29. *Cf. Gal. 3:28.
33. *In *Money Problems and Pastoral Care,* Paul Schurman offers some useful ideas on fiscal management for singles.
42. *At the Center for the Ministry in Oakland, California, during the years 1976–1980 a total of 206 pastors from a variety of Protestant denominations informally estimated that from 65 to 98 percent of the couples they marry have slept together prior to their wedding. The average estimate was 93 percent!
43. *For a comprehensive contemporary approach to sexuality within a Christian theological framework, see James B. Nelson, *Embodiment.*
48. *Ibid.
49. *Ibid., pp. 126–27.
49. †Ibid., p. 129.
50. *Based on data collected at the Center for the Ministry in Oakland, California, since 1970.
53. *Research findings have shown that in the United States married women have a lower level of mental health while single women have a far higher one. See Jessie Bernard, *The Future of Marriage* (New York: Bantam Books, 1972) for further discussion.
55. *Frank W. Kimper, "Musing on the Nature of Healthy Relationships" (Claremont, CA: unpublished article, circa 1973).
58. *Robert MacNeil, NBC-TV Network, May 30, 1981.
58. †"The Single Life" in *Christopher News Notes,* May 1980.
67. *John R. Landgraf, "The Impact of Therapeutic Marital Separation on Spouses in Pastoral Marriage Counseling." (Unpublished doctoral dissertation, School of Theology at Claremont, CA, 1973); see especially pp. 108–12 and Appendices B and C.

Annotated Bibliography

Adams, Margaret. *Single Blessedness: Observations on the Single Status in Married Society.* New York: Basic Books, 1976. This effective consciousness raiser attacks the notion that singlehood by choice is not healthy.

Antoniak, Helen; Scott, Nancy Lynch; and Worcester, Nancy. *Alone: Emotional, Legal, and Financial Help for the Widowed or Divorced Woman.* Millbrae, CA: Les Femmes Publishing, 1979. This book by and for women offers emotional support and legal and financial advice for single women.

Augsburger, David W. *Anger and Assertiveness in Pastoral Care.* Philadelphia: Fortress Press, 1979. This earlier volume in the Creative Pastoral Care and Counseling Series offers a useful, understandable approach to the release of tension and the constructive use of anger through assertiveness.

Bloomfield, Harold H.; Colgrove, Melba; and McWilliams, Peter. *How to Survive the Loss of a Love.* New York: Bantam Books, 1977. The bite-sized first-aid ideas in this "bedside companion" book are helpful in facilitating grief.

Bradley, Buff; Berman, Jan; Suid, Murray; and Suid, Roberta. *Single.* Reading, MA: Addison-Wesley Publishing Co., 1977. This reader on the joys of singlehood includes poetry and other items useful for singles' programs, plus a good bibliography.

Braudy, Susan. *Between Marriage and Divorce.* New York: Signet Books, 1976. This feminist journal is important reading for divorced singles, especially women.

Claremont de Castillejo, Irene. *Knowing Woman: A Feminine Psychology.* New York: Harper Colophon Books, 1974. This awareness raiser, written with subtlety, lucidity, and balance from a Jungian perspective, has significant chapters on "The Animus—Friend or Foe?" and "The Older Woman."

Emerson, James G., Jr., *Divorce, the Church, and Remarriage.* Philadelphia: Westminster Press, 1961. Helpful for persons who wrestle with sacramental or legalistic views of divorce as wrong.

Fisher, Esther Oshiver. *Divorce: The New Freedom.* New York: Harper & Row, 1974. Fisher's intelligent discussion of the use of groups for divorced singles is helpful in predivorce and post-divorce counseling.

Goldberg, Herb. *The Hazards of Being Male: Surviving the Myth of Masculine Privilege.* New York: Signet Books, 1977. This "male liberation" primer ought to be read by single men and male pastors; its chapter on "The Lost Art of Buddyship" is worth the price of the book.

Hyatt, I. Ralph. *Before You Marry Again.* New York: Random House, 1978. The "Do-It-Yourself Unraveling" exercises for divorced men and women are especially helpful for persons prone to remarry quickly.

Kennedy, Eugene. *Crisis Counseling.* New York: Continuum, 1981. This encyclopedic primer in crisis theory and methodology, written for the nonprofessional counselor, is neither pedantic nor boring.

Krantzler, Mel. *Creative Divorce.* New York: Signet Books, 1975. Singles who have suffered disappointment in relationships will find the "nine emotional traps" section especially worthwhile.

Lasswell, Marcia; and Lobsenz, Norman M. *Styles of Loving: Why You Love the Way You Do.* New York: Doubleday & Co., 1980. This potential "study guide" for a church singles group examines six basic styles of loving and their implications.

Miller, Jean B. *Toward a New Psychology of Women.* Boston: Beacon Press, 1977. A clear awareness raiser for men as well as women, clergy as well as laity.

Moustakas, Clark E. *Loneliness.* Englewood Cliffs, NJ: Prentice-Hall, 1961. This excellent counseling aid challenges the person blocking catharsis and the person living alone to make peace with solitude.

Nelson, James B. *Embodiment: An Approach to Sexuality and*

Christian Theology. Minneapolis, MN: Augsburg Publishing House, 1979. Traditional and nontraditional sexuality issues are both carefully set within a biblical-theological context in this scholarly and sensitive but highly readable treatise in theological ethics.

Oates, Wayne E. *Pastoral Care and Counseling in Grief and Separation*. Philadelphia: Fortress Press, 1976. This earlier volume in the Creative Pastoral Care and Counseling Series regards loss by death as the prototype of other significant losses and includes valuable discussions of divorce grief, rituals of separation, and postdivorce bereavement.

Ripple, Paula. *The Pain and the Possibility*. Notre Dame, IN: Ave Maria Press, 1978. Essential reading for divorced Catholics, the book will help all divorced persons with self-affirmation and healing.

Schurman, Paul C. *Money Problems and Pastoral Care*. Philadelphia: Fortress Press, 1982. This earlier volume in the Creative Pastoral Care and Counseling Series includes useful approaches to counseling single adults with respect to financial matters.

Stone, Howard W. *Crisis Counseling*. Philadelphia: Fortress Press, 1976. This earlier volume in the Creative Pastoral Care and Counseling Series is the best initial text for the pastoral crisis counselor.

Viscott, David. *Risking*. New York: Simon and Schuster, 1978. Singles who tend to "play it safe" will learn here the value of risking in order to grow, love, change, or decide.

Weiss, Robert S. *Going it Alone: The Family Life and Social Situation of the Single Parent*. New York: Basic Books, 1979. This is the best book available on single parenting.

Westberg, Granger E. *Good Grief*. Philadelphia: Fortress Press, 1962. This short, simple, forthright, and constructive book makes a fine handout for new singles, especially if singlehood has been unanticipated.

Zimbardo, Philip G. *Shyness: What It Is, What to Do About It*. Reading, MA: Addison-Wesley Publishing Co., 1977. Singles who have trouble with shyness, and the pastors who counsel them, would do well to read this definitive work on shyness.